Walks in the footsteps of

Rosamunde Pilcher

Published by Sigma Leisure – an imprint of Sigma Press, Stobart House, Pontyclerc, Penybanc Road, Ammanford, Carmarthenshire SA18 3HP.

British Library Cataloguing in Publication Data
A CIP record for this book is available from the British Library.

ISBN: 978-1-910758-46-5

Typesetting and Design by: Sigma Press, Ammanford.

Cover photograph: Carricknath Point © Sue Kittow

Photographs: © Sue Kittow, unless otherwise stated

Maps: © Sigma Press
Contains OS data © Crown copyright [and database right] 2019

Printed by: TJ International Ltd, Padstow, Cornwall

Walks in the footsteps of
Rosamunde Pilcher

Sue Kittow

Acknowledgements

To my loyal proof readers, in alphabetical order: David and Jenny Dearlove, Av Harcourt, Colin Ivens and Shelagh Smith.

To John Roberts for those all important grid references.

To Tony Foster for valuable tide and general seagoing information.

Many thanks to all who have come on walks with me – in alphabetical order – Steve Baldwin, Colin Ivens, Jo Knight, Fiona Saunders, Viv Simmons and Titch.

To the dear friends who accompanied me on these walks, pored over maps and helped keep me going: in alphabetical order: Steve Baldwin, Ursula Hold, Colin Ivens, Jo Knight, Fiona Sanders, Viv Simmons and Titch. And to all those who, for whatever reason, weren't able to accompany me – I know you were with me in spirit.

To Moll, for being her.

And to everyone for their ideas, inspiration and encouragement along this journey.

If I have missed anyone out, please forgive me.

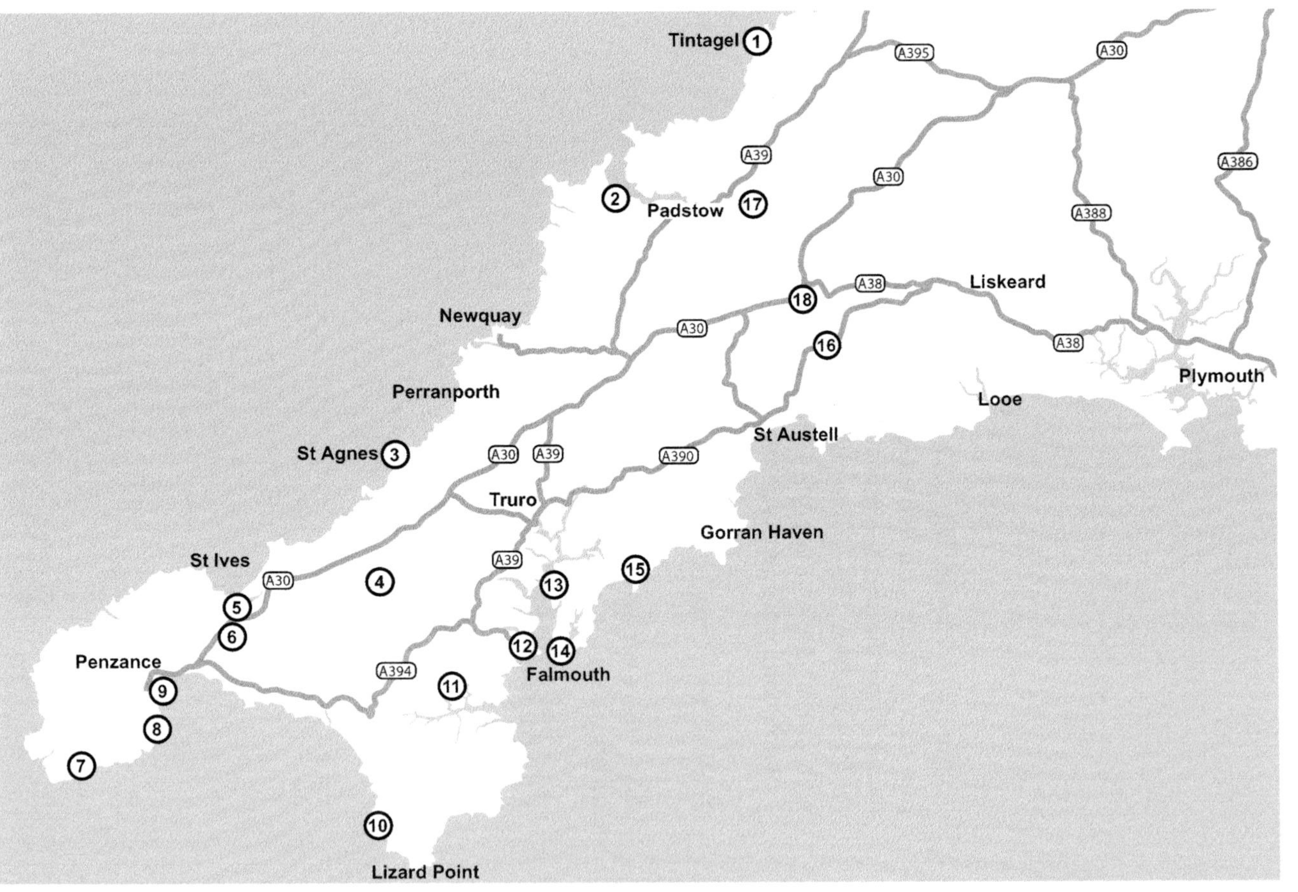

Tintagel 1
A395
A30
A39
A30
A386
2 Padstow 17
A388
A38 Liskeard
18
16
A38
Plymouth
Newquay
A30
Looe
Perranporth
St Austell
St Agnes 3
A30 A39
A390
Gorran Haven
Truro
St Ives
A39
15
A30 4
13
5
6
12 14
Penzance
A394 11
Falmouth
9
8
7
10
Lizard Point

CONTENTS

INTRODUCTION

Sadly Rosamunde Pilcher died on 6 February 2019, six months before this book was published.

I hope this will be a fitting tribute to an incredibly talented writer whose love of Cornwall came alive with every word of every story she wrote, set in her homeland.

I can't remember the first Rosamunde Pilcher novel I read, for she seems to have been part of my life for as long as I can remember. I must have been a young teenager, getting lost in her descriptions of Cornwall as a place of sun and beauty, of excitement and romance. I devoured my own copy of *The Shell Seekers* and was instantly absorbed into the story that is as relevant now as it was when she wrote it – no wonder this book was such a massive bestseller. A few years ago I was delighted to find a DVD of the film in a jumble sale – I have watched it often since, and loved every minute of it.

Several years ago Mr B and I were in Penzance, browsing in antique shops, when he bought me a copy of *The World of Rosamunde Pilcher* – a beautiful hardback book with colour plates, detailing her childhood, how she became a writer, and how important Cornwall was to her, as well as her adopted Scotland.

So imagine how excited I was when the editor of *Cornwall Today* asked me to interview her, in 2014. It was a telephone interview, as she was in Scotland, so sadly I was unable to meet her in person, but although approaching her 90th birthday, her mind was a lot sharper than mine, and we found we shared the same favourite walk, which I have featured in this book. This was one she did as a young girl, and one that I regularly walked on a Sunday afternoon having dropped my jazz enthusiast husband off at the Smugglers Inn at St Erth to attend his favourite jazz session. You may have gathered from this that I did not share his enthusiasm for jazz. Now, nine years after his death, the walk has very bittersweet memories for me.

I have interviewed many famous authors over the years, but that interview with Rosamunde Pilcher will stay with me forever. It was such a privilege to talk to a true Cornish author of such calibre and intelligence who, incidentally, went to the same school as my mother in Penzance.

Any Cornish resident – and many visitors, now – are accustomed to seeing German film crews around the county, filming her short stories for German audiences on a Sunday night. Many a time I have met German couples or families here while out walking, and nearly all of them have come here because of the Rosamunde Pilcher films. Or because their wives watch them!

When I visited Prideaux Place and met Prideaux-Brune, she had very happy memories of meeting Rosamunde Pilcher, and said that the film crew have visited so often they feel like part of the family. Since then over 100 films have been made at Prideaux Place, some featuring her husband and lord of the manor, Peter Prideaux-Brune. As a result, the house and gardens are extremely popular with many of our German visitors, as well as our English ones, and the family were the first to ask if they could stock this book when it's published – in German.

These books are not just for the walker – I frequently give talks to those who are not able to walk, for whatever reason, and those who live abroad. My sister-in-law in Vermont is one such example. For these reasons, I try to give a flavour of the season, the weather, what we saw and heard, tasted and smelt on our travels, so that those who aren't able to physically do the walks, can enjoy the journey and participate as armchair travellers. Similarly with the history of the area, and details of the books or locations involved – these add another dimension to what is essentially a walking guide, but I hope can also be read on its own as a book celebrating Cornwall's uniqueness.

These Rosamunde Pilcher films usually portray Cornwall at her best, and I hope that our visitors to this wonderful place I am lucky enough to call home, will have as much fun with these walks as we have. Your presence here is very welcome and we particularly enjoyed sampling the cafes we selected for you en route!

Sue Kittow
July 2019

GENERAL INFORMATION

- These walks vary in length, so take note according to how much time you have available.

- When out walking, wear appropriate footwear and clothing as weather conditions can change very quickly – rain, fog or even sunshine can descend at a moment's notice.

- Take a mobile phone with you, but be aware that there are many places without a signal, so tell others when and where you are going – and when you return.

- The cliff path is hazardous to dogs who may chase birds and rabbits etc., so keep dogs on a lead near the cliff edge.

- Cornwall is littered with mine shafts, so be careful.

- While the maps contained in this book are as accurate as possible, it is advisable to take the relevant Ordnance Survey map or use one of the OS apps on your phone.

- It's possible you may get lost, or want to just sit and admire the view – take food and water with you, particularly if you have dogs who may get thirsty.

- Respect crops and livestock – keep dogs under control near all animals especially sheep and cattle when their young are with them.

- Respect other people's land and please shut gates behind you.

- Please take all rubbish home with you if you cannot find a litter bin.

- If you are intending to walk on or near beaches, be aware of high and low tides – see following page.

Tides

When walking by the sea it is important to be aware of what the tide is doing. Always check the times of high tide before you set out and know whether it is coming in or going out during your walk. You can find tide times from local radio or in newspapers and many local shops sell tide tables.

The tidal range is much greater at some times than others. Spring tides occur every two weeks around the time of full moon and new moon. The difference between low and high water can be over 5 metres (16ft.) on Cornwall's south coast and 7.5 metres (21ft) on the north coast. Strong on-shore winds can increase the height of tide by up to a metre, especially if accompanied by low atmospheric pressure, usually associated with gales. The time between high and low water is roughly six hours. You are most at risk in the few hours after low water when the tide is returning: it comes in slowly at first but is at its fastest in the 3rd and 4th hours of the flood.

Neap tides, when the range is about half the maximum, occur in the weeks between spring tides. Most tide tables also show the height of high water next to the time – the bigger the number on the day of your walk, the higher the tide will rise.

While we're talking about the sea, just a short word on waves. The complex weather patterns that constantly run into our beautiful Cornish coast often set up wave patterns that cross at an angle to the underlying swell from some distant storm. These will occasionally combine to produce a rogue wave of up to twice the height of the regular waves. There are plenty of clips on- line showing what happens to the reckless when that happens. Don't be one of them!

Below are a few websites you may find helpful.

www.ukho.gov.uk/easytide/EasyTide/ShowPrediction.aspx?PortID=0005&Predicti onLength=7
The UK Hydrographic Office is the source of tidal data for all the other sites and limits its free information to the next 7 days.

www.bbc.co.uk/weather/coast_and_sea/tide_tables/10
The BBC list 16 locations around Cornwall and give you a nice little graph of tidal height.

www.newquayweather.com/wxcornishtides.php
Great local weather information. The tides times links you to the UKHO site.

www.cornwalls.co.uk/weather/tide_times.htm
The Cornwall Guide website also provides a wealth of other information for visitors.

www.tidetimes.org.uk/falmouth- tide- times
This site includes an option to order a printed copy of tide tables for the whole year.

WALK ONE
TINTAGEL

Rosamunde Pilcher's name has long been synonymous with outstanding entertainment, both for her novels – which have sold over 30 million copies all over the world – and for the ZDF small-screen adaptations of her works which are watched by around six million people in Germany.

The first ZDF Pilcher film, *The Day of the Storm* in 1993, was seen by over eight million viewers and since then over 100 have been made. Rosamunde Pilcher was born in Lelant, and says it all started here in Cornwall, "on the beaches, sitting on the rocks and making up little stories in my head, a long time ago".

Tintagel refers not only to the famous castle on an island but also to the small town on the mainland formerly called Trevena, or 'farm on a hill', both of which have spectacular views of the rugged north coast. There are many stairs from the bridge linking the island to the castle, but the view is breathtakingly beautiful, so well worth the trip, and the castle was used in the Rosamunde Pilcher film, *Argentine Tango.*

Tintagel is full of myths and mystery, and for centuries has inspired artists and writers who have associated it with the legend of King Arthur. He is said to have been born at the castle, while one of the caves on the beach was rumoured to have been Merlin's home.

Tintagel Old Post Office is also worth seeing and was also used in *Argentine Tango* when Valentina and Jack research Jack's new travel guide. Originally a 14th century farmhouse, this has a wonderfully wavy roof. Glebe Cliff and the ancient church of St Materiana are also a must, and there are many places to eat and drink in this cosy little town.

What you need to know	
Distance	Approximately 4 miles
Allow	3 hours not including refreshments
Suggested Map	OS Explorer 111 Bude, Boscastle & Tintagel
Starting point	Glebe Cliff NT car park. Grid ref SX 050 884
Terrain	Moderate/easy
Nearest refreshments	Trebarwith Strand; Tintagel
Public transport	Train station Bodmin Parkway 15.6 miles. 75 bus to Tintagel Visitor Centre. Also buses 95, 96 and 212
Of interest	Tintagel Castle, Tintagel Old Post Office, St Materiana Church, Trebarwith Strand, numerous beaches
Facilities	Trebarwith Strand, Tintagel

The Walk

One sunny morning in late September, Fiona, MollieDog and I drove into Tintagel where we turned first left past the Old Post Office, down Vicarage Hill, a steep lane signposted to the Church of St Materiana.

Materiana is also thought to have been known as Madryn, a 5th century Welsh Princess from Gwent in Wales, who preached in North Cornwall around AD 500. An oratory served by monks stood on this beautiful hilltop position in the sixth century, but was replaced by a Saxon stone church and the site was used as a Christian graveyard from the years 500– 700.

The present building is thought to have been built as a daughter church to nearby Minster (near Boscastle) where St Materiana was allegedly buried. The church dates to the late 11th century, although the tower is thought to be 13th century, whereas the north and south doors are Norman and the north porch is 14th century. There is also a Roman stone from the 4th century with the name Emperor Licinius, indicating there was once a Roman camp nearby.

Driving past the church on the left, we parked in the Glebe Cliff National Trust car park, and stood in amazement, enjoying the perfect views: on our right

The Old Post Office

St Materiana church

(north) we looked over to Tintagel Head and the Island, where we could see lots of visitors enjoying the superb views from Tintagel Castle. Looking south west, out over the wide sweep of Port Isaac Bay, we could see down to The Rumps and Pentire Point in the distance.

From the car park we followed the coastal path south which is gravelled here, and with the church on our right we walked past a picnic table and a cycle rack on our right, past a large boulder. It really was the most superb weather, with mackerel clouds drifting overhead, but out in Port Isaac Bay the sky was a clear, royal blue with only the hint of a cool breeze to remind us that autumn was approaching.

We passed the Youth Hostel on our right – "It's a fantastic place to stay", said Fiona, and looking at the view, it certainly is, particularly if you're a walker. (I would stay there but they don't allow dogs.) Out to sea we could see Gull Rock as we followed a slate lined path, while on our right the sea was gently boiling around the rocks, like an outdoor jacuzzi.

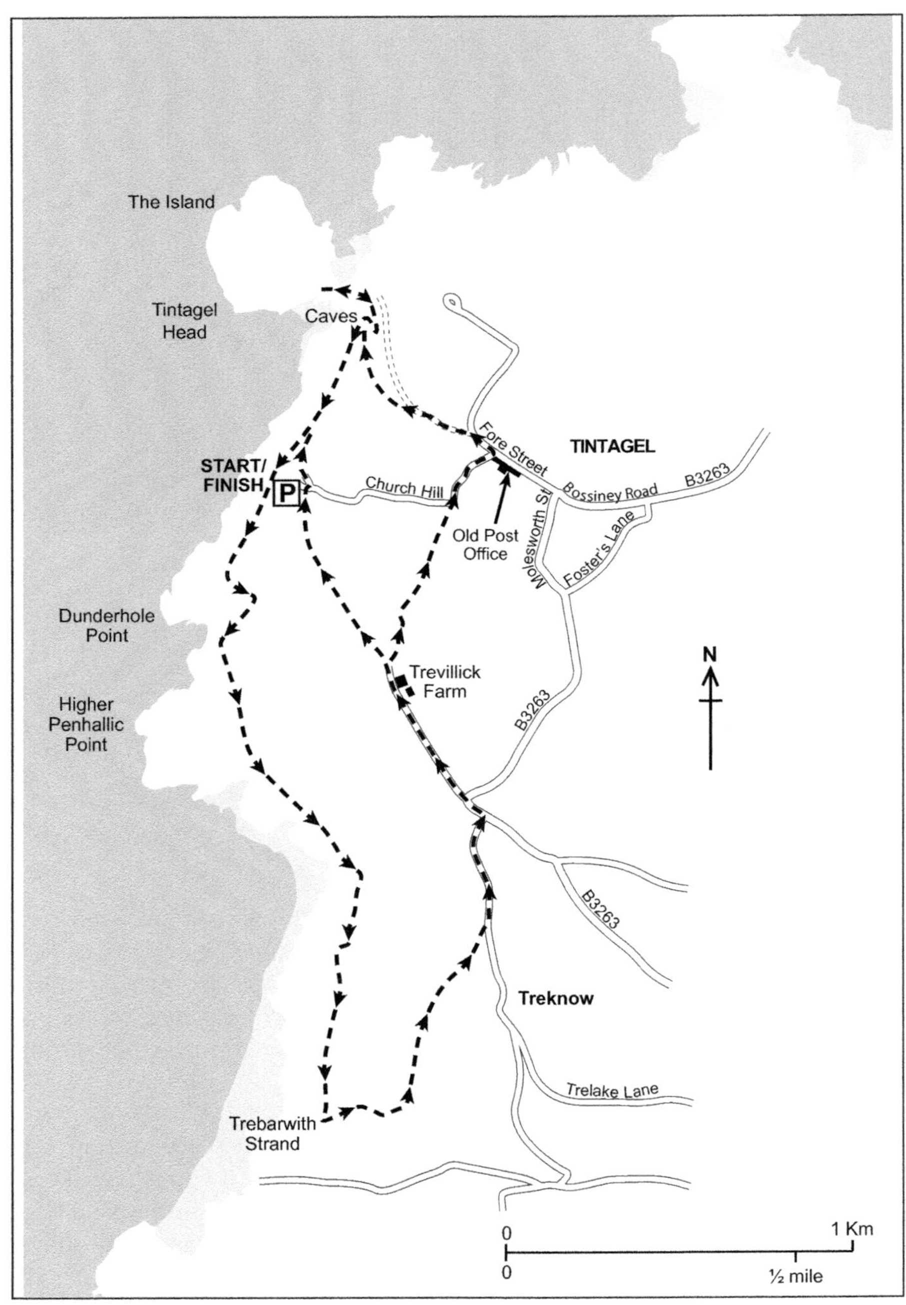

The Island
Tintagel Head
Caves
Dunderhole Point
Higher Penhallic Point
START/FINISH
P
Church Hill
Old Post Office
Fore Street
TINTAGEL
Molesworth St
Bossiney Road
B3263
Foster's Lane
Trevillick Farm
B3263
B3263
Treknow
Trelake Lane
Trebarwith Strand
N
0   1 Km
0   ½ mile

It was easy walking along here, so we were able to enjoy the spectacular geology – part of the cliffs here were pure slate, for there are nine slate quarries along this stretch of the coast where quarrying operated from the 14th century to just before the Second World War. Cutting the stone and loading it onto boats was very dangerous work, with men working round the clock. In 1889, three men vanished into the sea when the cliff face they were working on sheared off into the water below.

Passing through a wooden kissing gate, we looked down the coast and enjoyed the names along here – we passed Dunderhole Point, then Gull Point, and came to the headland of Higher and Lower Penhallic Point, from where we could look over to Trebarwith Strand. The beaches along here are beautiful too, revealed in all their golden glory as the tide receded – Bagalow Beach, Hole Beach, Vean Hole and Lill Cove, before reaching Trebarwith Strand and Port William, at the far end.

The sun sparkled and shimmered over this vast expanse of water, making us think we could have been in the Mediterranean but without having to travel so far. At this time of year there was very little vegetation in the hedgerows – lots of brambles and the last of the blackberries, and a lone ragged robin, as well as some bracken about to turn bronze.

View to Trebarwith

We passed through another kissing gate, meeting a lady with a Jack Russell and a lurcher, and climbing upwards we came to a stile then a National Trust sign indicating 'Bagalow', where the path turned inland for a while along a muddy track. The only sound was the murmur of the sea in the distance. Peregrine falcons breed along this part of the coast; they can reach over 200 mph when diving for prey, making them the fastest member of the animal kingdom.

A skylark bounced through the sky ahead of us, while a magpie darted towards a hedge, and looking down, lazy waves rolled back and forth trailing curves of froth in their wake. Coming to a slate stile, we walked past a very narrow stack of slate rearing up like a lone soldier. It is actually 80 foot high, rising from the remains of Lanterdan quarry which, along with West quarry, were once some of the largest quarries in North Cornwall. The stack was left behind as it wasn't of good enough quality to sell. Lanterdan Quarry is now owned by the National Trust and contains rare shellfish fossils and a rare mineral called monazite.

Passing another sign to Hole Beach we could see several people swimming in the sea and some, rather optimistically, trying to surf, though there wasn't enough wind to produce big waves – they rippled daintily along the sand like lace doilies.

Reaching the top of the hill, we began the descent down into the valley. This is quite a steep narrow path with high hedges on both sides, and very sheltered, so by this time we were walking in shorts and tee shirts. Looking

Lanterdan stack

down onto Trebarwith beach, we noted that it is dog friendly year round, and there were plenty of four legged friends enjoying the sand.

A huge bumble bee flew heavily over Fiona's head as we took a left fork, then we noticed a Red Admiral butterfly and the last of the blackberries amid the ivy clad banks, together with an unusual white and yellow vetch, like a wild wallflower. The path became rocky here, so it's important to wear footwear with good grip on the soles.

Reaching Trebarwith Strand, we noted the Port William pub at the top of the hill, which is very good and with stunning views, but we opted for the Strand Cafe down by the beach, where we sat outside with our coffee and shared a beautifully moist piece of carrot cake, which had walnuts and a lovely creamy topping. This little hamlet consists of a few cottages, a cafe, public toilets and a shop selling ice creams, buckets, spades and surfboards.

There was originally a small harbour at Port William which was used to export slate. The sandy beach here is completely covered at high tide but can be reached over the rocks when coming from Treknow. There are also lots of caves here if you enjoy exploring, and rock pools if you don't. Lifeguard cover runs from mid May until the end of September, but check online for exact dates.

Suitably refreshed, and after a quick explore of the beach, we retraced our steps up the hill, past a sign indicating 'Tintagel 2¼ miles'. We took a turning on our right to Treknow, and further on we took another right turning again signed to 'Treknow', just before a large pink house with tall chimneys up on our right, and a sign to 'The Bluff'.

Our walk was cheered by several Red Admiral butterflies, and a lot of trailing ivy in the hedgerows, while bracken was starting to turn a rusty colour and we heard a pheasant squawk in the valley below us. At a gateway we paused to look back down the valley and out to sea, which had turned a stunning rich, royal blue. We realised that we were walking in the footsteps of old quarrymen, and I thought that Rosamunde Pilcher would have loved this bit of history.

Coming to a tarmac drive, we walked along the ridge of the hill, looking down onto the village of Treknow on our right, while the hedges were crammed with the biggest, fattest blackberries we had seen. A solitary white bindweed flower peeked out from the hedges, while ebullient hydrangea flowers burst forth in delicate shades of coral, lilac and copper blue.

At the end of this tarmac drive we walked straight ahead past a Bed & Breakfast on the left called Trenowan and crossed over to a pavement on the right hand side of the road. Coming to a junction with the B3623, we followed a sign on the left to 'Tintagel ¾ mile'. Shortly after that we took the turning signposted to the Youth Hostel and walked down a quiet lane with fields on either side and in the distance we could just see the church tower of St Materiana.

Sparrows chirped as they flew over the hedgerows, the sun beat down from a clear blue sky and a gentle breeze cooled us as we walked – it really was a perfect afternoon. Coming to a junction with three public footpath signs, we took the one on the right with a T-junction sign next to it. This led down a drive with grass in the middle, and cows and horses on either side. Walking up a few steps to climb a stile, we noted a sign saying 'Please put Bar Back' and from here the footpath skirted the field. We had to climb over several other wired stiles, which meant carrying Moll over each one, so take note if you have a large, heavy dog.

We passed rather beautiful ducks and geese in a field on the right, and later on, after several more slate stiles, came to a field of sheep, so put Mollie on the lead. We followed a well trodden path through this field which led to a gate where we saw a sign indicating Village straight ahead, so we walked down the lane, then uphill into Tintagel village. This is a lovely leafy, quiet lane with a beautiful old vicarage on the right with a huge stone wall surrounding it – it turns out this is now holiday accommodation and looks a stunning place to stay. Further on was a house with gabled windows, and the car park to the Cornishman Inn. It seems extraordinary that we were just outside busy Tintagel, where this is such an oasis of peace and quiet.

Reaching the village, we found the Old Post Office with its amazing wavy roof. The building was originally built over 600 years ago, as a farmhouse. Its last use was as a post office during the 1870s and today you can explore five rooms. The building is owned by the National Trust and is a Grade I listed building.

Being a gardener, Fiona was entranced by the cottage garden. "Look", she said. "The trees are the most fabulous autumn colour". On asking about the planting here, it appears that there is something for every season of the year – daffodils and snowdrops in spring, tulips and bluebells in April and May, and a selection of geraniums in June.

After this we decided to have a drink in the pub opposite and it was very pleasant relaxing in the afternoon sun, drinking ginger beer, and watching the world go by. We walked back along the main street, then retraced our steps by following a sign on the left to 'Parish Church and Glebe Cliff'. We walked back down Vicarage Hill, and continued up the other side until we finally came to the church and then back to the car park at Glebe Cliff.

It was now time to visit Tintagel Castle, so we turned right onto the coastal path (instead of left, previously) and walked to the castle, which was built in the 13th century by the Earl of Cornwall. However, pottery remains of a Roman settlement dating back to the 5th or 6th century have been found here, and there was also evidence of a royal site, with much trade of pottery and glass being imported to Tintagel from the Mediterranean countries.

The 12th century writer, Geoffrey of Monmouth, named Tintagel as the birthplace of King Arthur, in his book *History of the Kings of Britain,* though it's not known why. King Arthur was supposedly ruler of Britain, Ireland and large parts of Europe, so this gave him international fame. Legends continued to grow, and in 1480 William Worcestre cited Tintagel as Arthur's conception and birth place. The name 'King Arthur's Castle' first appeared in 1650, and by this time it was firmly established in local folklore and legends.

It seems that these associations led Richard, Earl of Cornwall, to build the castle here in the 1230s. Long after the castle became a ruin, its supposed links to King Arthur and Merlin have kept interest in Tintagel very much alive: Victorian tourists loved the idea that there was a Celtic king based here at the time of King Arthur, and that he and his knights were at war with Anglo-Saxons trying to invade Cornwall.

Having explored the castle, and enjoyed the spectacular views, we continued along the coastal path to the next headland of Barras Nose, and made the most of the views out over the Atlantic. Tintagel has been named a Site of Special Scientific Interest (SSSI) because of the erosion along the cliffs which has produced a set of bays, caves, blowholes, stacks and headlands. Barras Nose is an important geological site, where the rocks were changed by earth movements some 400 million years ago. The intense pressure and heat turned some of the slate into schist: a coarse grained rock in layers of different minerals that can still, like slate, be split into thin plates. "Look", I said. "The slate looks like it's almost fallen into folds along here", – another sign of the heat from millions of years ago.

Marvelling at nature, which is even more magical than the legends of King Arthur, we returned along the coastal footpath towards the car park, minds full of Merlin, King Arthur and their place in Cornwall today. Fiona looked out over the bay and smiled. "The weather couldn't have been better today, could it? Just like it is in the Rosamunde Pilcher films."

I nodded. I could smell the salt in the air, feel the breeze on my face and felt so relaxed in the September sunshine. The colours are always clearer and more vivid at this time of year, with the long afternoon shadows. How could anyone not love Cornwall on a day like this?

PADSTOW, CAMEL ESTUARY AND PRIDEAUX PLACE

Home of the Prideaux-Brune family
featured in many Pilcher films

The Prideaux family origins go back to the 11th century and are said to descend from such diverse characters as William the Conqueror, King Edward I and Queen Eleanor of Castile, with Jane Austen also being a close relation. Since the house was completed in 1592, fourteen generations of the family have lived at Prideaux Place.

The filming of *Coming Home* here has been a great draw for Pilcher fans worldwide, as have the other productions made for German television such as *Flowers in the Rain, The End of Summer, The Long Weekend* and *The Red Dress* (for a longer list of films see the end of this walk).

The house itself, surrounded by 40 acres of gardens and its own deer park, is a mix of Elizabethan, Strawberry Hill Gothic and Georgian architecture. The 18th century outbuildings in the Stable courtyard are also well worth a visit, housing Britain's oldest cannon, Roman coins and also a recording of all the filming that has taken place here.

I was fortunate enough to meet Elisabeth Prideaux-Brune who took me for a guided tour of this fascinating house. "The Prideaux family got the land in 1525, started building the house in 1588 and completed it in 1592," she told me. "My husband, Peter, was born and grew up here so he's been here for 74 years. Sadly his first wife died very young, but we married in 1988 so I've been here for 30 years." She smiled. "When we came here, every room in the house was under scaffolding because of wet rot, dry rot etc."

The first records of the gardens at Prideaux Place date from the 1730s, when Edmund Prideaux landscaped hedged walks and built a classical temple, a grotto and a small stone arbour. Over the past twelve years, Prideaux-Brune and her team have been working hard to restore the gardens to their former glory. The gardens are now beautiful and peaceful, providing a welcome haven from the bustle of nearby Padstow.

"When we came it was just a house with trees," said Prideaux-Brune. "I said to Peter, 'I'm dying to start on the garden,' and he said, 'no, we must do the house first'. So we redecorated all the house open rooms and some bedrooms and about 12 years ago, he said, 'Would you like to start on the garden?' And I said, 'Would I?!'. It was a complete jungle so I thought the only thing to do was start at the house and work round and it's been such fun to do: such a challenge. It's a work in progress, which gardens always are."

"Seventeen Pilcher films have been filmed here so far, including the 100th one. Peter Prideaux–Brune, a retired barrister fond of cigarettes and teddy bears ("we have forty in our bedroom," Prideaux-Brune told me) has often taken a cameo part in the films. "So far he's been a chauffeur, a gin taster and a coroner," she said.

The family have definitely noticed a rise in the number of German visitors since filming started. "The first film was in 1994 I think," Elisabeth told me. "We get around 32,000 visitors a year and around 80% of those are coaches with Germans and some Swiss and Austrians, but we are also getting a lot of individual visitors who come by car."

To help with their visitors, they now employ German speaking staff. "We have around twenty German speaking guides," Elisabeth said. "Some days there are up to seven coaches but quite a few of our German speaking guides live here which is helpful."

Apart from the licensed cafe, which features fresh, local food, and amazing cream teas, the deer park is another draw – in particular seeing these wonderful animals being fed. "That occurs at around 3pm every afternoon," she told me. "It's supposedly the oldest enclosed herd in the country apart from the Royal Parks."

But there's no doubt that the house itself is the main feature. "We do need visitors – the upkeep is horrendous, like a sponge," says Prideaux-Brune. "As soon as one bit's mended, the next bit starts to fall down." Looking at it from the outside, you'd never know, and seeing the inside of the house is a real privilege. "The visitors seem to love the fact that it's a family home with lots of photographs and it's lived in, unlike a National Trust house, so it has a family feel to it."

What you need to know	
Distance	3.5 miles
Allow	2 hours 15 minutes plus time for refreshments and visiting Prideaux Place and gardens
Suggested Map	OS Explorer 106 Newquay and Padstow
Starting point	Link Road car park, outside Padstow. Grid ref: SW 916 752
Terrain	Fairly even
Nearest refreshments	Prideaux Place and Padstow
Public transport	Plymouth City Bus number 11A – Padstow to Bodmin Parkway station via Wadebridge; First Kernow bus number 56 – Padstow to Newquay. Nearest railway station Bodmin Parkway
Of interest	Prideaux Place, gardens and deer park, Padstow, Tregirls Beach and St George's Cove
Facilities	Padstow, Prideaux Place

The Walk

One Friday in August, Viv, Titch, MollieDog and I drove up to Padstow, through the town, avoiding the town centre, and followed signs to Prideaux Place. On the outskirts of the town, we parked in the Link Road long stay car park – at time of parking, price was £4.90 for 3-4 hours.

In the far corner of the car park, by the public toilets, we followed a sign to the town centre and walked down a steep winding path. Near a stone building on the left was another town sign so we continued down steep steps until we reached Church Lane and walked past the back of the Golden Lion pub, which is the oldest pub in Padstow, dating back to 14th century. Turning right, by the side of the Golden Lion in Lanadwell Street, we reached the square which was humming and throbbing with summer visitors, then arrived at the harbour.

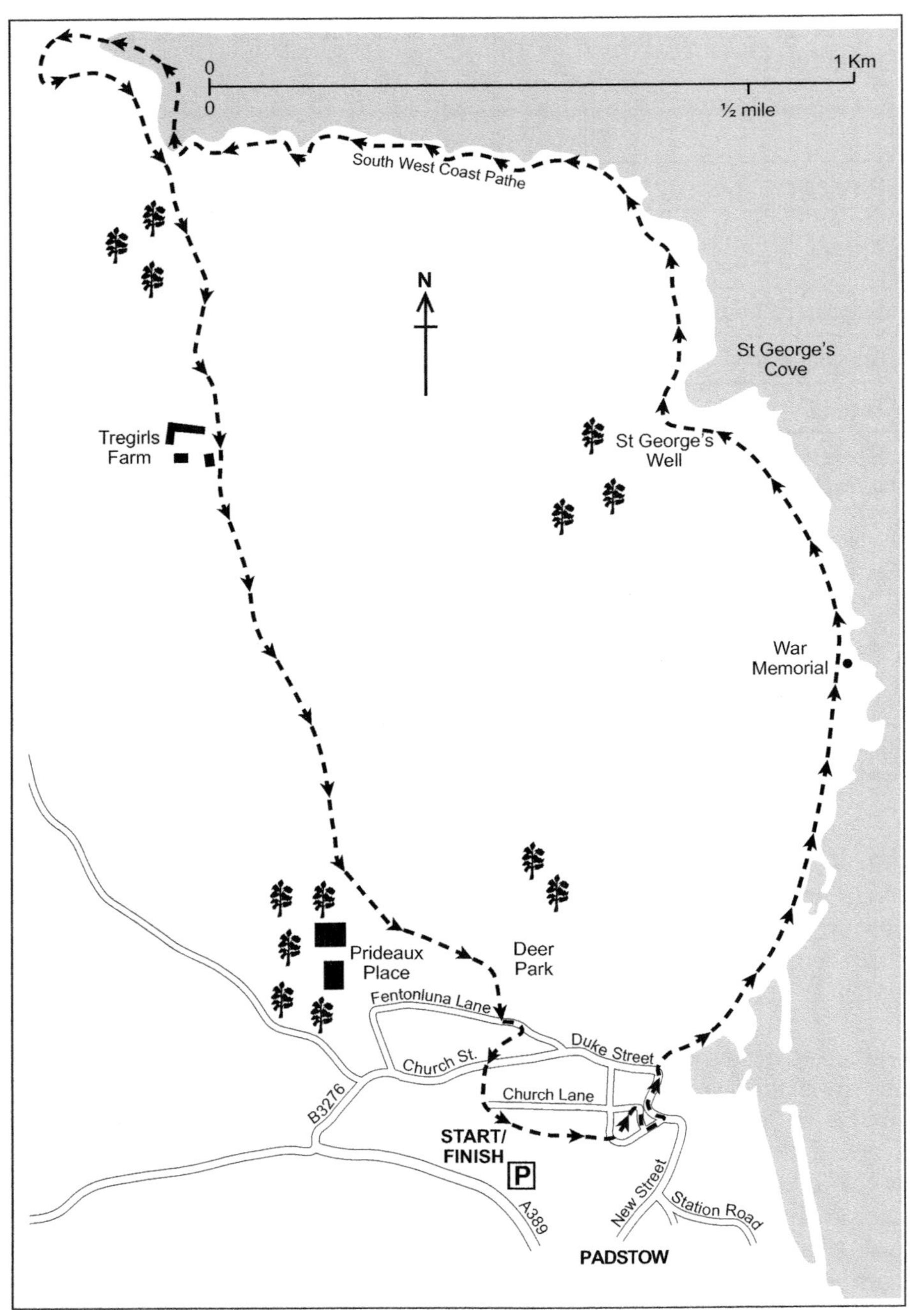

1 Km
½ mile
South West Coast Pathe
N
St George's Cove
St George's Well
Tregirls Farm
War Memorial
Prideaux Place
Deer Park
Fentonluna Lane
Church St.
Duke Street
Church Lane
B3276
START/ FINISH
P
Church Lane
New Street
Station Road
A389
PADSTOW

Everywhere we looked people were eating – ice creams, cream teas, pasties, chips and sandwiches, all eyed by crafty looking, hungry seagulls. Other visitors sat on the harbour benches watching the cluster of boats in the harbour, while others visited the many restaurants and shops owned by the famous chef Rick Stein. He also owns a pub, cookery school, several holiday cottages and 40 guest rooms around Padstow, earning it the nickname, 'Padstein'.

On 1st May every year, Padstow is famous for the annual Obby Oss (Hobby Horse) celebrations, one of the oldest May Day traditions in Europe, that dates back to the Celtic Beltane festival. The celebrations begin at midnight and by dawn the town is decorated with bunting, greenery, flowers and a maypole. Two groups of dancers make their way through the town singing the traditional song, with one member dressed as the Oss with a black cape under which they try to catch young women. This was supposed to bring them luck via fertility.

The two Osses are known as Old and Blue Ribbon, the latter devised by the Temperance Society to try and discourage drinking alcohol, though this has not been successful! Padstonians and visitors come from far and wide to attend the May Day celebrations which is the biggest event in the Padstow calendar.

Padstow is still a working port – although not as busy as in the 19th century, when there were six shipyards. In the 1880s when wooden ships were replaced with iron, shipbuilding declined, but by the end of the 19th century, Padstow was visited by east coast trawlers who made the town the centre for their winter fishing. In 1899 the railway opened and this enabled the export of fish, so by the 1920s there were still over 100 fishing boats

Padstow

working out of Padstow. When the railway closed in 1967, the fishing industry took a dip but recovered in the 1980s and nowadays the fishing fleet is smaller but still active.

Padstow faces the Camel Estuary and has been used as a natural harbour from 2500 BC, when it linked Brittany to Ireland from Fowey. Many of the buildings in Padstow are from the 18th or 19th centuries, but the shops and houses near the harbour date from mediaeval times.

We walked round the harbour to the north side (left), past Abbey House which is supposedly the oldest house in Cornwall. "There was once a tunnel from the house out to sea, or some say to the monastery up the hill," said Viv – she lived here thirty years ago so is somewhat of an expert on the matter. "There is also an Elizabethan ghost that haunts this house, climbing the stairway from the cellar

Abbey House, Padstow

and moving silently along the oldest passage in the house." She paused for effect. "From 1938 to 1981 this house was occupied by a widow who would stand looking out at the harbour, waiting for her husband to return from sea. In fact, he'd been killed in a car crash soon after they bought the house."

I shivered, and we left Abbey House behind, then passed a Tourist Information Centre opposite, by Padstow Rowing Club and where the road splits, we took the left path, near more public toilets, up towards the war memorial. Visitors wanting to go over to Rock on the ferry should take the right hand path – we could see queues of people waiting for the ferry.

Climbing northwards up towards the Meadow, we were able to let the dogs off the leads so they could run free, and at this point the sun came out, bleaching the sand at Rock a paler gold, and turning the sea a rich shade of royal blue.

As we walked, dodging visitors, we reflected that the best time to visit places like Padstow is in winter – or at least autumn, when it's less busy, but today it was interesting to see just how many people had flocked to this stunning part of Cornwall. Were we really walking in Rosamunde Pilcher's footsteps, I wondered – had she come here on a family outing, taken the ferry over to Rock, perhaps, and had a picnic there?

We could hear the low diesel thrum of the ferry engine as we walked up to the war memorial, then, coming to an open gate with a stile on the right, we went straight ahead, following the coastal footpath, with Harbour Cove, known locally as Tregirls beach, ahead of us. This is a vast area of sand that at low tide stretches out towards Doom Bar and merges with the other beaches, so it's possible to walk around Gun Point to St George's Cove over the sand.

Looking ahead we could just see the daymark at Stepper Point, peeping over the hill. This 40 foot stone tower, known as the Pepper Pot, was built for navigation purposes as it's 240 foot above sea level and is visible from 30 miles. Straight ahead of us were the cottages at Hawker's Cove, behind which Viv used to live: when she was a younger woman, she would walk this route back from work in the evenings. "I saw two badgers fighting along here one night," she said. "That was the only time I was afraid – I couldn't think what it was at first."

The field next to us was full of stubble, and a few crows pecked away at the ground, while seagulls wheeled gracefully above us on unseen thermals, and in the distance we could hear the keening cry of an oyster catcher. The islands off Cornwall have colonies of breeding puffins, and from April to July, you can often see guillemots and razorbills that look rather like penguins.

We continued walking along the coastal footpath, which is pebbly but inlaid with years of trodden sand, while clumps of old man's beard sprouted from the hedges. From the beach we could hear people calling their dogs, who barked in response: there are various paths leading down onto the sand, but beware of the tide that comes in extremely quickly and can leave you stranded.

Coming to a waymark sign to St George's Cove, we could have left the path and headed for the beach, but we decided to keep to the coastal footpath. St

Cottages above Tregirls beach

George's Well, one of many holy wells in Cornwall, is supposed to be off the path above the beach. In early times, sources of water were very valuable, especially to travellers, and the Celts and Romans believed the wells had great healing powers.

It was low tide when we walked, and we could see the massive sand bank of Doom Bar ahead. According to local legend, the Mermaid of Padstow fell in love with Tom Yeo, a local lad who thought she was a seal and shot her. As hell hath no fury like a woman scorned, the mermaid summoned a huge storm, wrecking all the ships in the harbour. Not satisfied with that, she threw a massive sandbar across the river to endanger all future sailors trying to venture into Padstow. Doom Bar is still there, and the cause of many a shipwreck over the years.

The sandy path wound round with grasses on either side, and everywhere we looked, we noticed tiny sea snails clinging onto the rough blades of grass. Finally we found a path that took us down a gentle slope onto the beach. "I know there are plenty, but I need one where the drop isn't too steep because of my ankle," said Viv, who broke it last year very badly – as a result she's understandably very nervous.

We crossed Tregirls Beach, enjoying the feel of the fine silver sand between our toes, and then opposite found a corresponding pathway over the purple grey slate rocks where we turned right onto the coastal footpath. Passing round the back of several houses, one of which was the old lifeboat station, (it has now been relocated to Trevose Head) we came to a private slipway with several boats, and followed several signs to the Rest a While tea garden – I was starting to feel hungry so this cheered me no end.

We passed what looked like an old kennel outside with KEVIN written on it which made me smile – although as Viv pointed out, this could have been used for his mail, then through a car park, round the back of more houses, and finally came to another sign to the Rest A While teashop 50 metres up the path on the left. Open 10.30-4.30 April to October, depending on weather and demand.

This teashop boasts one of the best views in Cornwall, and having reached here via a steep narrow path, I couldn't disagree. The sands of the Camel Estuary stretched before us, edged with ripples of white laced waves, and following the estuary around, we could see Rock, then Padstow in the distance. It was truly the stuff of picture postcards, and I would return here any day. The tea shop is also unique in that it consists of a hatch into the house, from where food is ordered and dispensed. Seating is via outdoor tables and chairs, but there is no shelter, so if it is raining they may not be open.

However, we sat there in sunshine along with other families with dogs, and found that when our excellent lemon drizzle cake arrived, we were also given a bowl of dog biscuits! The portions are huge and all looked home made – the scones were the size of horse's hooves, so a cream tea would satisfy the most hearty of appetites. We opted to share a piece of cake and I was in two minds about whether we should have a slice each but having seen the huge chunk that arrived, I was glad we were sharing. The cake was lemony, moist and delicious. A real treat!

The bungalow that Viv had lived in was next door to this teashop, separated by a large fence, so I was able to peer over and see the huge garden that housed many geese. "I wonder if they're descendants of the ones we kept," said Viv whimsically.

Refreshed and rehydrated, we walked back down the path and retraced our steps along the coastal footpath while admiring some of the boats on the slipway – I was having withdrawal symptoms from not sailing. Instead of cutting back across the beach as we had on the way out, we continued along the path until we reached a wooded area near St George's Cove, and carried on walking along a small boardwalk and over a stream. This led up a few steps, through a kissing gate and into a huge field with a path on to the left, round the boundary of the field.

Pausing to admire the bountiful and huge sloes, we walked around the field, looking back over the estuary at the cluster of cottages at Trebetherick, then the steep mound of Brea Hill, then St Enodoc church and golf course stretched round and in front of us. Ahead of us, westwards, on the right, we could see a farm which we hoped was Tregirls Farm, and were very thankful we'd had that cake to keep us going.

The path deviated to the left, away from the field, as we walked over another boardwalk, came to a waymark sign and turned right up the hill (turning left would have led us back to the beach). From here we walked up the hill which took us to Tregirls Farm. Looking back we could see the pale sands in the distance, the cottages where we'd had tea, Polzeath and Pentire Head, then all the way round to Rock and Padstow.

Continuing up the hill we came to Tregirls Holiday Cottages, offering self catering accommodation at the farm: lovely old cottages that I would love to stay in. We carried on walking up the hill which led to a tarmac road where we turned south. This road had very high hedges on each side which protected us from the wind and fat spots of rain that had started to drop, while sycamore and oak trees bent over to the left due to the prevailing south westerly winds. Further along, we came to a beautiful archway which marked the edge of the Prideaux estate, and as we grew closer to Prideaux Place itself, noticed the deer being fed in the deer park. We stood and gazed at these beautiful animals which is quite a sight, seeing them all gathered together.

It was at this point that I was lucky enough to meet Prideaux-Brune, and spent a fascinating hour talking and then exploring the house. I could happily have spent many more hours there, but the dogs were getting restless, so it was time to move on. Leaving the house by the main entrance, we walked back towards the main road, turned left and retraced our footsteps back to the car park. "What an incredible place," said Viv, echoing my thoughts. "And what a gem of a place to use for filming – no wonder so many of the Pilcher films are shot there. I wonder whether Rosamunde Pilcher went there?" She paused, to put up her hood – it was raining steadily by now. "How could anyone not love Prideaux Place?"

Pilcher Films shot at Prideaux Place			
1994	End Of Summer	Das Ende Eines Sommers	(Ffp)
1999	A Long Way Home	Der Lange Weg Zum Gluck	(Ufa Films)
2005	Magic Night	Sommer Des Erwachens	(Ffp)
2007	Winds Across the Sea	Winde Uber Dem Meer	(Ufa Films)
2011	Stolen Summer	Gestohlener Sommer	(Ffp)
2011	The Mystery of The White Dove	Das Geheimnis Der Weissen Taube	(Ffp)
2011	Stormy Seas	Gefahrliche Brandung	(Ffp)
2011	Engaged and Confused	Verlobt, Verliebt, Verwirrt	(Ffp)
2012	The Woman on the Cliff	Die Frau Auf Der Klippe	(Ffp)

Prideaux Place

ST AGNES HEAD AND CHAPEL PORTH

Cornwall's mining heritage

The coastline between Chapel Porth and St Agnes Head features as a backdrop in many episodes of the Rosamunde Pilcher films, with the disused mine engine of Wheal Coates as a poignant reminder of Cornwall's industrial heritage.

In *The Prime of Life*, Ellen is featured at St Agnes Head during a car trip; Lilian has an accident on St Agnes Head in *Wings Of Cornwall*, while some diving scenes with Holly were filmed at St Agnes Head in *The Woman on the Cliff*, and the stone hut where Holly and Owen visit after the ride on the beach is also near St Agnes Head.

Hang gliding scenes from *Old Heart Not Rust* were filmed here, and in *Evita's Revenger*, Anna and Peter have a picnic here. It was also the scene in *Trust is Good, Love Better*, where Rod and his uncle Jeff have a test drive, and in *Election Promises* and *Other Lies*, Abbey and Greg find that their love for each other is still alive – this also takes place at St Agnes Head.

Wheal Coates

It also features in *Love, Thieves, Diamonds* when Marian passes Rick a box of letters that she never sent him.

Once you visit this area you will see why it is so popular – this shows the north coast at its most dramatic, with spectacular views that will literally take your breath away. No wonder it's such a popular area for filming and walking, and There is so much space here, you feel you are getting a glimpse of the real Cornwall.

What you need to know	
Distance	4 miles
Allow	2 hours including refreshments
Suggested Map	OS Explorer 104 Redruth & St Agnes
Starting point	St Agnes Head car park Grid ref: SW699 512
Terrain	Few steep hills, uneven ground in places
Nearest refreshments	Chapel Porth cafe
Public transport	87 and T2 buses from Newquay, Perranporth, Truro and Redruth
Of interest	St Agnes Head and Beacon, Chapel Porth, Wheal Coates mine and others
Facilities	Chapel Porth beach

The Walk

One blustery, bright Monday morning in April, Jo, MollieDog and I drove to Chiverton Cross roundabout and took the exit marked B3277 St Agnes, then after about 200 yards we came to the Three Burrows roundabout and turned right, signposted St Agnes. After about 3 miles along a straight road, we came to the outskirts of St Agnes and another small roundabout where we took the first left onto Goonvrea Road. We followed this road for just under a mile where the road curved round to the right onto Beacon Drive.

We drove along Beacon Drive for another mile curving round from west to north, and came to a layby on the left, with the Beacon on the right. Just before

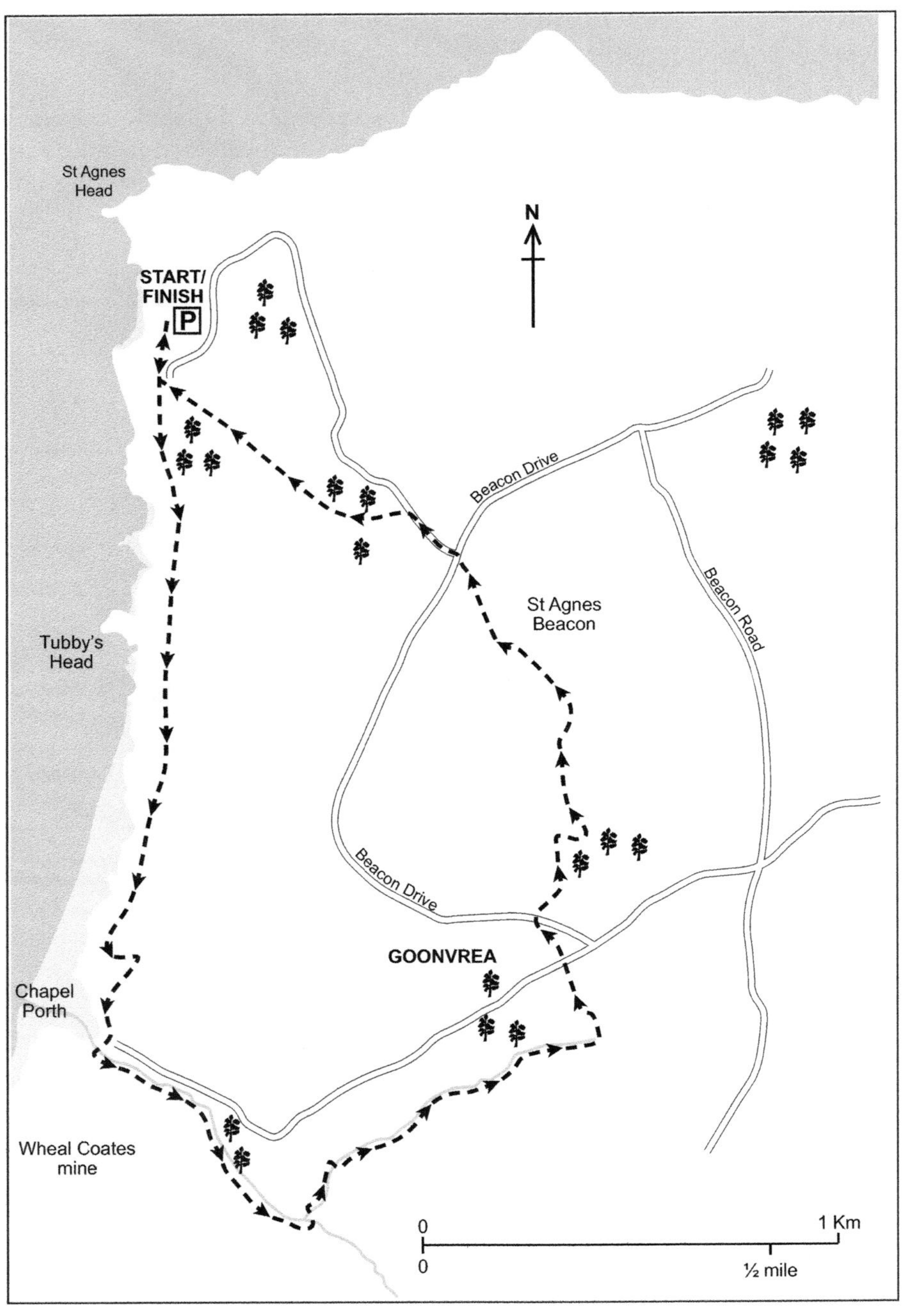

St Agnes
Head
START/
FINISH
P
N
Beacon Drive
Beacon Road
St Agnes
Beacon
Tubby's
Head
Beacon Drive
GOONVREA
Chapel
Porth
Wheal Coates
mine
0
1 Km
0
½ mile

the layby is a turning on the left which we drove down and followed the road round until we saw the Lookout Station on our right. A little further on we parked in a large car park on the right – at the time of walking it was free.

From the car park, we headed south, and followed the footpath down towards Towanroath Engine House, looking out over a teal coloured sea with huge Atlantic rollers bearing in, spray flicking off the top of the waves in excitement. "Just think, it's Canada over there," said Jo, as we looked out over the huge expanse of churning blue sea and a horizon stretching into infinity, while a brisk wind kept us from talking too much.

A large breeding colony of kittiwakes (a member of the gull family) live on St Agnes Head. These birds are recognisable by their black legs and black wing tips, and in spring and summer the birds form colonies on cliffs or rock stacks. From August they move offshore to feed, surviving only on fish, unlike their cousins the herring gulls. Kittiwakes have been declining in some areas, possibly due to overfishing.

We took the lower coastal path which led us past a quarry area – "this is a perfect sheltered spot for a picnic," said Jo. Continuing along the footpath we enjoyed the views south along the coast past Porthtowan and Portreath and on to Godrevy Point and St Ives in the distance. "You can usually walk from Chapel Porth to Porthtowan," said Jo, "but the structure of the beach has changed so that's not possible at the moment."

It was low tide on the day we walked, and expanses of virginal golden sand spread out below us, framed by proud, thundering waves, and dark rocks rising out of the sea – a truly spectacular sight and typical of this north coast.

Further along, we opted to take the higher path which led to the upper buildings of Wheal Coates Mine which worked from 1815-1914, on and off, producing 335 tons of copper and 717 tons of tin. These buildings include the Stamps and Whim (winding) Engine House, which kept water out of the shaft 600 foot below and were used to hoist and crush tin ore. There is also another chimney stack and a calciner furnace, used to remove arsenic and sulphur from the tin. Both of these have been well looked after by the National Trust since the 1970s. Walking among these buildings, you can almost hear the clangings and bangings of the mine, the men shouting to each other, and imagine the world as it was then, producing all those tons of tin and copper to be exported.

Below us, perched on the edge of the cliff, was the Pumping Engine House on Towanroath Shaft, one of the most photographed engine houses in Cornwall, which has also been well preserved. It was built in 1872 to house a pumping engine which kept the Wheal Coates shafts dry. The pumping shaft was sunk to 185m which is well below sea level.

Surface mining for ore has taken place here since mediaeval times, but records of underground mining date from 1692, because of flooding and problems bringing ore to the surface. In 1828 steam-driven pumping and winding engines were introduced to enable the mine to reach 135m deep. At its peak, Wheal Coates employed 140 miners with tin being transported on the tramways and shipped from Portreath, Hayle, Trevaunance Pier in St Agnes and Truro.

There are many footpaths along this part of the coast, but most lead down to Chapel Porth and soon we found ourselves heading downhill into a steep valley where we were out of the brisk wind, which was a relief. The path winds down and round and MollieDog, who knows this walk well now, trotted on ahead leading the way until eventually we arrived at Chapel Porth, its name set in white stones on the opposite bank.

A mediaeval chapel and Holy Well dedicated to St Agnes were originally sited in an enclosure above the gully to the right of the beach. The well remained

Towanroath Shaft

until 1820 but the stones from the chapel were used elsewhere locally. Every April, and ending on 1st May, the Bolster Day is held at Chapel Porth, with giant puppets re-enacting the Cornish legend of St Agnes, a young girl who kills the fierce giant Bolster, who was rumoured to eat children and overcame Sir Constantine and many local heroes. If you visit the Driftwood Spars pub at nearby Trevaunance Cove, one of the local ales is named Bolster's Blood.

There is a small National Trust car park at Chapel Porth, and the beach has a dog ban from Easter to the end of September, so we headed to the cafe, which has several tables outside. As it was windy, we both had the most delicious French Onion Soup with garlic bread, but we could have had a wonderful selection of hot and tasty dishes such as Croque Monsieur, or their famous Hedgehog ice creams which have to be sampled to be believed! I would add that no hedgehogs were used in the making of these delicacies, but they are ice cream smothered in clotted cream, nuts and all kinds of deliciousness.

Path to Chapel Porth

We sat inside the shelter out of the wind, while Moll padded between everyone, trying to look under nourished, in the hope of getting some food. She was unlucky this time but bore no ill will and was eager for the next part of the walk.

From here we followed the stream up the valley of Chapel Coombe, past a sign saying Porthtowan 1½ miles, and enjoyed seeing the pussy willow emerging with its cheerful pale green fronds. On the right, above us, were the remains of Charlotte United engine house which produced 23,000 tons of copper ore in its time.

Chapel Porth

There's a dense jungle of holly, gorse, and willow trees on the left and further on we came to a junction with yellow and blue waymark signs so we followed the yellow ones pointing left, over the stream and past a couple of stalls selling plants, books and flowers. We turned right after the second stall and continued ahead till the junction with Chapel Porth Farm where we forked right up a rough, rocky path up the hill.

There were many pine trees towering overhead, and a hamlet of houses on the left while black caps, willow warblers and chiff chaffs called from the bushes on either side of us – when it's sunny you can also see dragonflies and damsel flies.

At the top of this track we came to a junction by a house and garden, where we turned left through a kissing gate and walked past a house called Firs Dene with the stream on our right and the first bluebells and primroses. This lane wound past Willow Cottage, while we could hear the summer rumble of a lawnmower in the distance.

At the top of this lane we crossed a road, heading uphill past daffodils, forget-me-nots, a lavender bush and lots of alpines. We followed the Public Bridleway sign which led along another rough track up to a holiday complex, with the path on the right. At the top we came to another junction where we turned left into Beacon Drive then first right, which leads up to St Agnes Beacon looming ahead of us.

Ignore the first path on the left which comes to a dead end, but continue to the next junction where you can go straight ahead up to the Beacon, or turn left which takes you along the lower outskirts of the Beacon, which is what we opted to do as it was so windy.

Between two and five million years ago, St Agnes Beacon was an island bounded on the west by a wave-cut platform about 400 feet above modern sea level. A wave-smoothed cliff and pebbles and boulders were found at the level of the road which now circles the north west side of the Beacon.

Today the old sea floor shoreline is covered by thick layers of 'china clay' and sand of various colours, which are still extracted in the present-day quarry. In the past the clay was used to stick candles to miners' hard hats and to the walls of the mines.

In the past St Agnes Beacon has been used as a burial and ceremonial site, a military lookout post and early warning system, and as a place of recreation. The trig point at the top of the Beacon has a topographic plate showing places of interest, and the views from here are spectacular, all the way up to Trevose Head in the north east, and St Ives in the south west.

We continued walking, enjoying the views down the coast and out to sea – Bawden Rocks to the north is also known as Man and his Man, and Cow and Calf. Further on we came to a large area of the Beacon that had been burnt by a huge fire – the twisted, arthritic stubble wound out of the scorched earth like something from a horror film, and the wind howled round the telegraph poles, adding to the eerie atmosphere.

This path finally emerged back at a junction with Beacon Drive and opposite the layby where we'd turned down earlier. We crossed the road here and headed back along the road leading down to St Agnes Head. It's hard to imagine that in the Second World War, part of the land here was covered by Nissen huts, bungalows and even a theatre. The area was known as Cameron Camp and was first used by the Royal Artillery as a Light Anti-Aircraft Practice Camp.

From 1943-44 American army units used this camp before being sent to France, and after the war, the bungalows housed local families until more council houses were built in the village.

Opposite an old sentry hut, we turned left along a sign that confusingly says Private, next to a yellow waymark sign. This path meanders through rough ground, then we climbed over a long stone stile and walked along with a field on the left where there are often wedding marquees in the summer.

Heading towards the Lookout Station at St Agnes Head, we made our way along various paths until we came to a large information board of the area and this led back to the car park and our car.

This is one of my favourite walks, and one that I often do if I'm feeling unhappy – the stunning views and dramatic coast here never fail to lift my spirits. I did it on Good Friday this year, when we started off in rain, but climbing up to the Beacon, the clouds lifted, as did our spirits, and the sun shone for the rest of the walk. So next time you see a sun filled backdrop in one of the Pilcher films, remember that it really can be as beautiful in real life.

But it's best to experience it to believe it. In whatever weather, you won't be disappointed.

GREAT FLAT LODE

Another part of Cornwall's mining heritage

Rosamunde Pilcher was very proud of her Cornish roots, even if mining did not feature heavily in her books. But Cornish mining heritage is an essential part of the past, present and future of Cornwall, and this walk takes place in one of the most densely mined areas of the county.

During the boom of Cornish mining, many new estates were built, including Tehidy, the seat of the Basset family. John Francis Basset rebuilt the mansion in 1861, due to the huge income he derived from local mines: his yearly income from the Dolcoath and South Frances mines was about £20,000 – that's approximately £860,000 today.

Another wealthy Cornish landowner connected to this walk is Lord Francis de Dunstanville, one of the most successful mineral lords in Cornwall. The Carn Brea monument was erected in his honour, and this features later in this walk.

When the copper mines were closing, around 1860, a 'lode' of tin ore was discovered to the south of Carn Brea in an area that had previously worked copper deposits. Most veins of mineral were nearly vertical, but this two mile long lode was gently sloped, hence its name 'Great Flat Lode'. It follows part of the Basset Mine Tramway which was built to carry tin ore from the mines along the side of the valley for processing at Wheal Basset Stamps. The remains of the last tin smelter in Cornwall can be visited near Carnkie.

Mining was the main industry in this area in the 18th and 19th centuries and when a licence was granted in 1832 for South Wheal Basset (which became Wheal Basset), the mine was an instant success, making the Basset family very rich. Huge copper reserves were found at quite shallow levels and by 1880, over 128,000 tons of copper ore had been extracted. Under this were huge tin reserves in the Great Flat Lode.

In the late 19th century, these tin mines became some of the most profitable, supplying over 90,000 tones of tin concentrate, until the mines closed in around 1920. Since then, the area has remained undeveloped, so you can see wonderful examples of Cornwall's finest remains of engine houses, tin dressing floors and other mining structures.

This is a circular route with some steep sections, travelling through farmland, old mine sites and heathlands. The starting point is South Wheal Frances, which had been worked since the 1700s and is so named because Lady Frances Basset granted the lease of the mine in 1834 and by 1891 68,000 tons of copper ore and nearly 7,000 tons of tin ore had been extracted.

What you need to know	
Distance	6 miles
Allow	3.5 hours including coffee stop
Suggested Map	OS Explorer 104 Redruth & St Agnes
Starting point	South Wheal Frances car park. Grid ref SW 681 393
Terrain	Footpaths, a few steep hills
Nearest refreshments	The Croust Hut cafe https://www.thecrousthut.co.uk
Public transport	Bus 442 from Camborne, then walk from the Countryman Inn at Piece
Of interest	South Wheal Frances and other mines; Carn Brea Castle and Carn Brea Monument; King Edward Mine Museum; Shire Horse Farm and Carriage Museum
Facilities	The Croust Hut cafe

The Walk

One brisk, bright Friday, Fiona and I set forth with MollieDog from Four Lanes, heading north west on Little Gregwartha towards the B3297, then turned right onto the B3297. From here we turned left into Loscombe Road, then turned left onto Filtrick Lane and South Wheal Frances car park was on our right.

Walking through the centre of the car park, we found a metallic information board and turned right onto the path running behind this. Reaching a fork at a waymark, we kept right and followed the path to a road which we crossed by a sign indicating Great Flat Lode. Walking along here, we passed a big granite block with a notice saying Dismount Here, and further on we came to the Basset Mines Tramway tunnel (1908, rebuilt in 1997) as part of the Great Flat Lode trail.

The Basset tramway was built to take ore from the shafts at South Wheal Frances and Wheal Basset to the stamps for crushing and the dressing floors. The trams were originally horse drawn but a steam locomotive was added during one of the modernisation and extension programmes.

There was a lot of mine wasteland on our left and an enclosed mine shaft on our right. Arriving at a junction we turned left, downhill, and looked up to see a wonderful view of Carn Brea opposite, standing proudly at the top of the hill and Carn Brea Castle next to it. The weather was perfect – sunny but with a cool breeze that was good for walking. Our cheeks were chilled by the cold air, but it was invigorating as we strode along, past gorse bushes with golden flowers, and dessicated bracken lining the hedges.

Carn Brae castle

Reaching another junction with a road, we turned right and walked into the village of Carnkie while a blackbird sang clearly above us. Reaching Carnkie Methodist Church, we turned right and followed the road past some cottages to a track on the left, by a telephone box and a red letterbox.

N
Carn Brea Village
Carn Brea Castle
Carn Brea
Brea
Penhallick Road
Loscombe Road
START/ FINISH
South Wheal Frances Car Park
P
King Edward's Mine
0   1 mile
0   1 Km

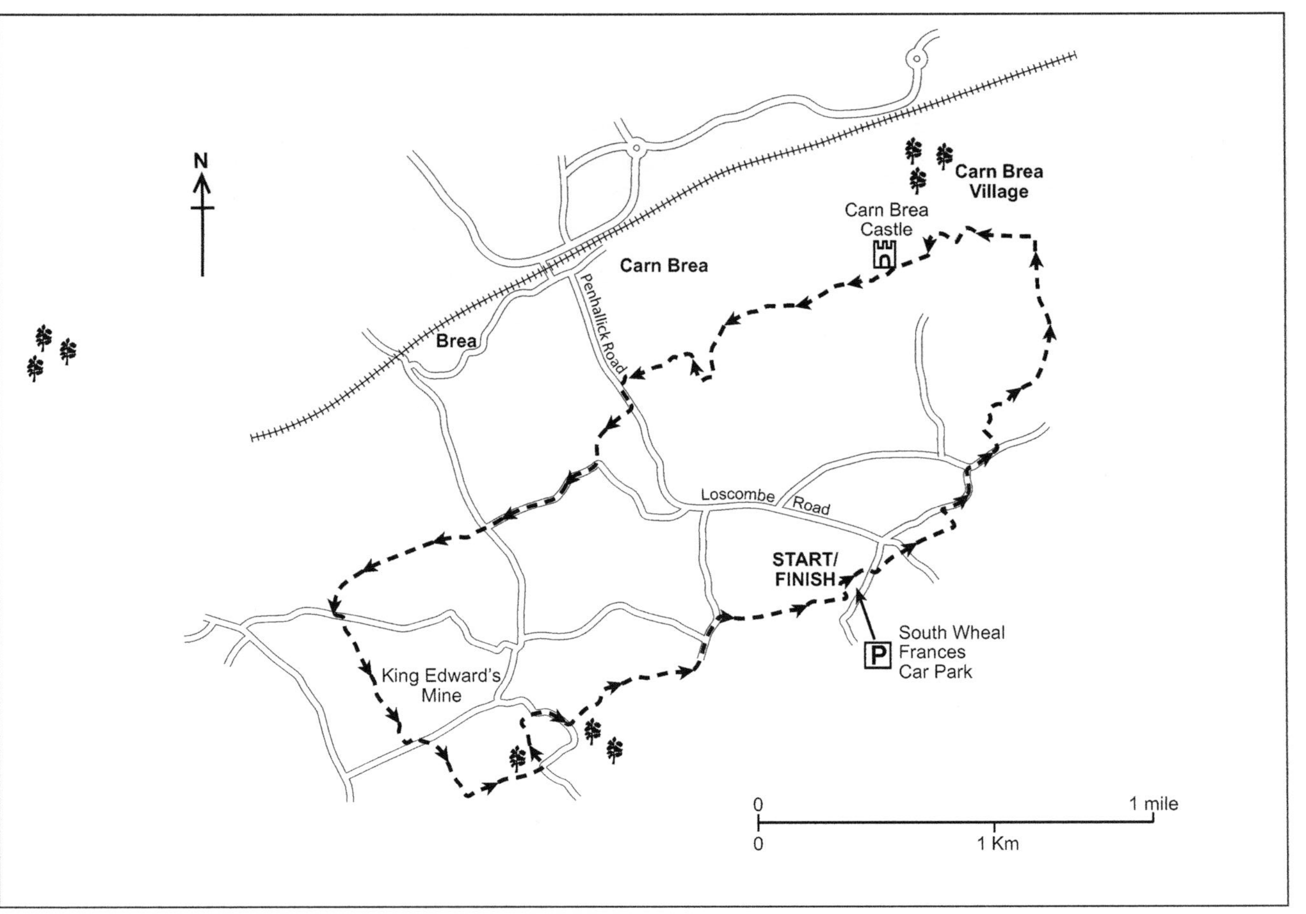

46

This track led past a car park at West Basset Stamps and, further on, to a cattle grid which can be bypassed through an adjacent kissing gate. Evidence of mining was all around us, with engine houses and chimneys peeping over hedges and from behind cottages. "I wish we could have seen all the mines working," said Fiona. "It must have been incredible."

At a fork in this potholed path, we continued straight on over another cattle grid then passed Karpan cottage on the left, with a lemony coloured camellia whose blooms had bruised and faded. We enjoyed wonderful views of the valley below us, scattered with more mine workings and a riding centre on the right, but very little signs of habitation otherwise.

The gnarled hawthorn trees were covered in gritty lichen - a sign of pure air, apparently, and we followed a pale blue waymark sign indicating straight on. Walking past a few more cottages, we noticed how loudly the birds were singing from hedges covered in scrub and gorse, while Cornish stone walling peeped through from layers of emerald green moss and other vegetation. On the right, we could see the sprawling industrialisation of Redruth to the north east.

At another junction of three paths, we took the middle narrow, stony path with granite boulders strewn along the way, leading steeply uphill towards Carn Brea Castle. A chapel dedicated to St Michael was built on this site in the 14th century, and later rebuilt as a hunting lodge for the Basset family in the style of a castle in the 18th century. Between the 1950s and 1970s the building lay derelict, but was renovated in 1980 and is now used as a restaurant, with wonderful panoramic views over St Ives Bay and the coast around Portreath. As a result, the castle is an important landmark for shipping, and a lease from 1898 stipulates that the tenant of the building must keep a light burning in a north facing window.

Keeping to the left of the castle, we came to a small car park and followed a concrete path, strewn with more granite boulders, and noticed Carn Brea monument in front of us. We came to a larger car park and took a small path on the right which led up towards the monument, just as the sun came out

Tor near Carn Brae

revealing skies of deep, clear blue which illuminated the views all the better.

On the side of Carn Brea monument is inscribed "The County of Cornwall to the memory of Francis Lord de Dunstanville and Basset A.D. 1836" who lived at Tehidy, in the parish of Illogan, and was a Cornish nobleman and politician, a member of the old Basset family. As he grew older, he was part of a group petitioning the House of Lords against slavery in 1828.

We continued towards the granite boulders, or you can follow the path along the left of them and head out over the moorland weaving your way through granite outcrops – this particular mass of granite is known as the Tregonning outcrop and stretches out to Porthleven in the south.

Carn Brae monument

Walking straight on, westwards, we came to a large boulder where we followed the left hand path towards another granite outcrop, and a stony path downhill to the left of it. We then turned right through the bracken heading down towards a small farm, and ended up on a track with a granite cross and a white-washed cottage – Burnt Cottage, Higher Tregajorran – on the left with a grassy track to the left of the building towards a telegraph pole.

Here was a path that followed steeply downhill past a holly tree with dark, glossy leaves, and steep hedges of bracken and brambles on either side. At a junction with two public footpath signs, we turned left, past a house and large conservatory and followed the drive round to the road. Here we turned left, along the main road from Pool to Four Lanes, until we reached a pavement on the left hand side.

Reaching a row of tiny cottages, opposite No 9, we crossed the road to find a track with a Public Footpath sign and walked along smelling wild garlic on either side and noticed the first bluebell leaves, while a crow cawed in the trees above us. "The joy of these walks are that they take you places you'd never normally go, and discover all kinds of things," said Fiona, as we walked past more cottages, from which dogs barked loudly.

Looking out over the countryside, all that can be seen is miles and miles of moorland, old mine workings, and horses grazing in fields – and yet this isn't far from the urban sprawl of Redruth.

Reaching a lane we turned right and continued past West Carnarthen Farm, then Harley Farm and over a small road bridge to a junction. Here we crossed a road and took a really steep tarmacked path uphill, meeting a lad who struggled up pushing his bike. At the top of this hill we emerged onto a track and continued on, past various farms and turned left to reach another lane.

At another junction we turned left and walked towards an engine house, looming over us, then just before it, we turned right onto a bridleway marked Great Flat Lode and continued along here until we reached a road. The sun cast lovely long shadows as we walked, and we enjoyed the fabulous views over fields and moorland and met several other dog walkers.

Just as I was beginning to fantasise about a cup of coffee, suddenly, in the middle of nowhere, we came upon the Croust Hut Cafe, open 10-4. "Hurry!" I said, as it was 3.40pm, so we rushed inside – dogs welcome – to the cafe which is round the back of the King Edward Mine Museum which opens from April 30th to end of October.

In 1897 an abandoned part of South Condurrow Mine was taken over by the Camborne School of Mines for a combination of training and commercial production, and renamed King Edward Mine in 1901. In 1987 a group of volunteers turned the unused mill complex of King Edward Mine into a museum where machinery has been restored to working as it would have done in the early 20th century.

There is a sign outside the cafe telling the visitors that the mining landscape of King Edward Mine is part of the World Heritage Site and as well as the important archaeology and architecture here, the legacy of tin and copper mining is evident in the ecology. Wildlife recovery is part of the landscape and cultural heritage. A beautiful piece of artwork next to it refers to the transformation from industrial wasteland to recovery.

"Isn't it amazing?" said Fiona – and sure enough, it is. The Croust Hut is made of wood and glass, is light and airy and was full of afternoon sunshine on our visit. The staff were friendly, the coffee very good and the menu looked so tempting, that Fiona decided, "I must bring Mum here – she'd love it."

We shared a piece of banana, cranberry and orange cake which was incredibly light and full of fruit – really delicious. The food is made from local produce where possible, and we determined to come back for another visit.

Fortified, we retraced our steps back to the path and turned left where we reached the road and the main entrance to the King Edward Mine Museum and car park, though as we walked in January, the museum wasn't open. We crossed over the road and on the left found another sign to the Great Flat Lode where we were surrounded by mining wasteland and a reminder of how once this area was so rich and is now one of the poorest parts of Cornwall.

Walking past a farm, we turned right at a fork and climbed uphill and at the top we reached another fork and turned left. At the bottom of this path we saw another public footpath sign and turned left over a stile and crossed a field heading towards an engine house. This field was very churned up and muddy due to the wet winter so it took us a while to get over the ground and reach another stile the other side.

From here we followed a path onto a grassy track in front of Wheal Grenville, Fortescue shaft. This was sold several times during the mid 19th century as profits were falling from copper and tin reserves. However, by 1881 the mine was so profitable that new engine houses were built, the remains of which can be seen today. The smaller chimney on the pumping engine house further along is due to a lightning strike in 1897.

Wheal Grenville

At the end of this path we turned right past a farm with very noisy collies. We then reached a small road at the end where we turned left by the next sign to the Great Flat Lode. This path led over a small concrete bridge, with the clearest water I've seen for a long time. Walking further, we reached a sign on a gate to the Shire Horse Farm and Carriage Museum which seemed shut, so we turned left onto the track which led to a tarmacked section which in turn led past some mining cottages and to a junction.

We followed the Great Flat Lode sign ahead until we reached another track opposite Thursday Cottage on the right. This led past more engine houses of South Wheal Frances which was amalgamated into South Frances United in 1892 and then with Wheal Basset into Basset United Mines in 1895 and these contained all the major tin mines on the Great Flat Lode. The area was later redeveloped and new buildings were added, but in 1918 the mines were finally closed and all the machinery sold for scrap.

These magnificent buildings look like roofless cathedrals in their elegance, standing proud against the skies with the odd rook flying above. It's well worth exploring here – there is an information board telling you more of the history of this fascinating place. The old mine workings are silent ghosts, bearing the stamp of much industry, engineering and hard work, and you can see areas where copper has leaked through in blue stains onto the surrounding granite.

Walking ahead, we came to a waymark sign and turned left past the Great Flat Lode sign, and finally returned to the South Wheal Frances car park where we started off. This walk will show you a very different side to Cornwall than the more picturesque areas, but it is nonetheless a true picture of how things were, when Cornwall was at the forefront of world mining.

LELANT TO CARBIS BAY

Rosamunde Pilcher's favourite walk

Rosamunde Pilcher's father, Charles Scott, was a Commander in the Navy and stationed in Hong Kong and Burma. As married couples weren't encouraged to bring up children in the Colonies, Mrs Scott returned to Cornwall with her first daughter, Lalage, who was then ten, and rented a cottage in St Ives. Rosamunde was born in Lelant on 22 September 1924 and grew up in The Elms, a large house near Lelant station with a rambling garden, perfect for children to explore. This was where she grew up, and began writing at the age of seven.

Many of Mrs Scott's friends were painters and authors and she became a member of the Arts Club of St Ives. As a result, the girls were always painting

The Elms

or working on a play or, when not being creative, they picnicked on the beach, enjoying the Cornish life outdoors.

Once she left school, Rosamunde went to secretarial college then got a job in the Foreign Office. But she admits being bored to tears, and enlisted in the Women's Royal Navy Service to serve in the Second World War. After two years in Portsmouth she was sent to Ceylon. From here she sent a short story to *Woman and Home* magazine, and in the summer of 1946 the story was published and she received fifteen guineas.

In 1946 many people returned to St Ives from the war, and there was much celebrating. At one of these parties, Rosamunde met Graham Pilcher, a young Scottish officer who was staying with family while recovering from severe war injuries. They married in December 1946 at St Uny church in Lelant, and shortly afterwards moved to Dundee, Scotland, as Graham was director of Jute Industries, the family business. They had two daughters and two sons, who eventually produced fourteen grandchildren.

Rosamunde's first book was published in 1949 under the pseudonym Jane Fraser, and she published another ten novels for Mills and Boon under that name. But in 1955 she started using her own name and *Secret to Tell* was published.

When Rosamunde first started writing, she said that it was a refuge from daily life, and saved her marriage. Her breakthrough novel was *The Shell Seekers*, published in 1987, which made her one of the most successful female authors of the time. This novel features an elderly British woman named Penelope Stern Keeling, who has problematic relationships with her grown up children and the very touchy topic of inheritance; an age old story of how money and greed can cause such terrible problems. *The Shell Seekers* sold more than five million copies worldwide and was made into a play and TV programme, available on DVD.

In 1996 her novel *Coming Home* won the Romantic Novel of the Year Award, but in 2000 Pilcher retired from writing and was made an Officer of the Order of the British Empire in 2002.

The German national TV station Zweites Deutsches Fernsehen (ZDF) has produced over 100 of her stories for TV beginning with *Day of the Storm* and these are some of the most popular programmes on German TV. Both

Rosamunde Pilcher and the director, Claus Beling, were awarded the British Tourism Award in 2002 for promoting tourism in Cornwall and Devon.

Rosamunde's happy memories of Cornwall are evident from her many books, in particular *The Shell Seekers*. Her son, Graham Pilcher, is also a novelist, and lives at Zennor, near St Ives.

In 2014 I was fortunate enough to interview Rosamunde Pilcher for *Cornwall Today* magazine. Unfortunately it was by phone, so I didn't get to meet her in person, but it was a memorable interview, and despite being in her early 90s, she was as bright and intelligent as a 20 year old! I asked if she had a favourite Cornish walk, and she said that she loved the walk from St Uny church, over the golf course to Carbis Bay. This was one she often did with her dogs, and she never tired of it.

Many years ago my husband would go to the Smugglers Inn at St Erth, Praze, renowned for its jazz on Sunday lunchtimes. Not being such a jazz fan myself, I would drop him off, then Moll and I would go adventuring. This was my Jazz Widow Walk and has remained one of my favourites ever since. It's reassuring to know I'm in such good company.

What you need to know	
Distance	**3.5 miles**
Allow	**2 hours**
Suggested Map	**OS Explorer 102 Land's End, Penzance & St Ives**
Starting point	**Layby outside St Uny church. Grid ref. SW 547 376**
Terrain	**Few steep hills**
Nearest refreshments	**Duckie's Cafe, Old Foundry Chapel, Hayle Badger Inn, Lelant**
Public transport	**St Ives Branch Line from Lelant Buses 1, 239, A2, A17 and T2 from St Ives**
Of interest	**St Uny Church, West Cornwall Golf Course, The Elms, Lelant**
Facilities	**Badger Inn, Lelant, Carbis Bay Hotel**

The Walk

One sunny morning in March, Ursula and I travelled down to Lelant, stopping off at the excellent cafe in the Old Foundry Chapel in Hayle.

The Old Foundry Chapel is well worth a visit, housing some quirky and interesting shops in the former chapel and schoolhouse. You can choose between vintage, art, antiques and jewellery shops as well as fashion, second hand books and beauty outlets, so there really is something for everyone here.

We drove southward out of Hayle, along the Hayle Estuary, on the B3301 towards St Ives. At the Badger Inn in Lelant, we drove down Church Road, and continued until we reached a parking area for several cars outside St Uny church. There is a public footpath sign indicating Carbis Bay 1¾ miles pointing to the left (west), so we walked along the footpath, which is the St Michael's Way, with the church on our right.

In the Middle Ages, Lelant was a sea port, but when the estuary silted up, lost the trade to St Ives. The first recorded spelling of Lelant was in a document dated around 1170 when it was named Lanata. The church here is thought to have been built in the 15th century, with some Norman features, but earliest records are from 12th century. This church was apparently also used to store smuggled goods.

Coming to a sign that we were approaching a golf course, we continued down towards Porthkidney beach and were met with the beautiful sight of Godrevy lighthouse across Hayle beach to the north east, in the distance. The sky was blue on this March day and out of the stiff north easterly breeze the sun was welcoming and warm on our faces. You could see why this was Rosamunde Pilcher's favourite walk – not just for her childhood haunts, but because of the sheer beauty of miles of almost white sands, the river Hayle running into the sea which was a deep blue with snow white surf, and the dunes crowning everything.

Heading west and keeping the golf course on our left, we came to a junction where we could have walked straight ahead to Porthkidney East beach but we followed the well marked path round to the left through the dunes, with golfers enjoying the sun and dogs barking excitedly on the beach below us. Passing a lookout station on our right, we continued along this path until we turned right over a railway bridge and then left at the other end.

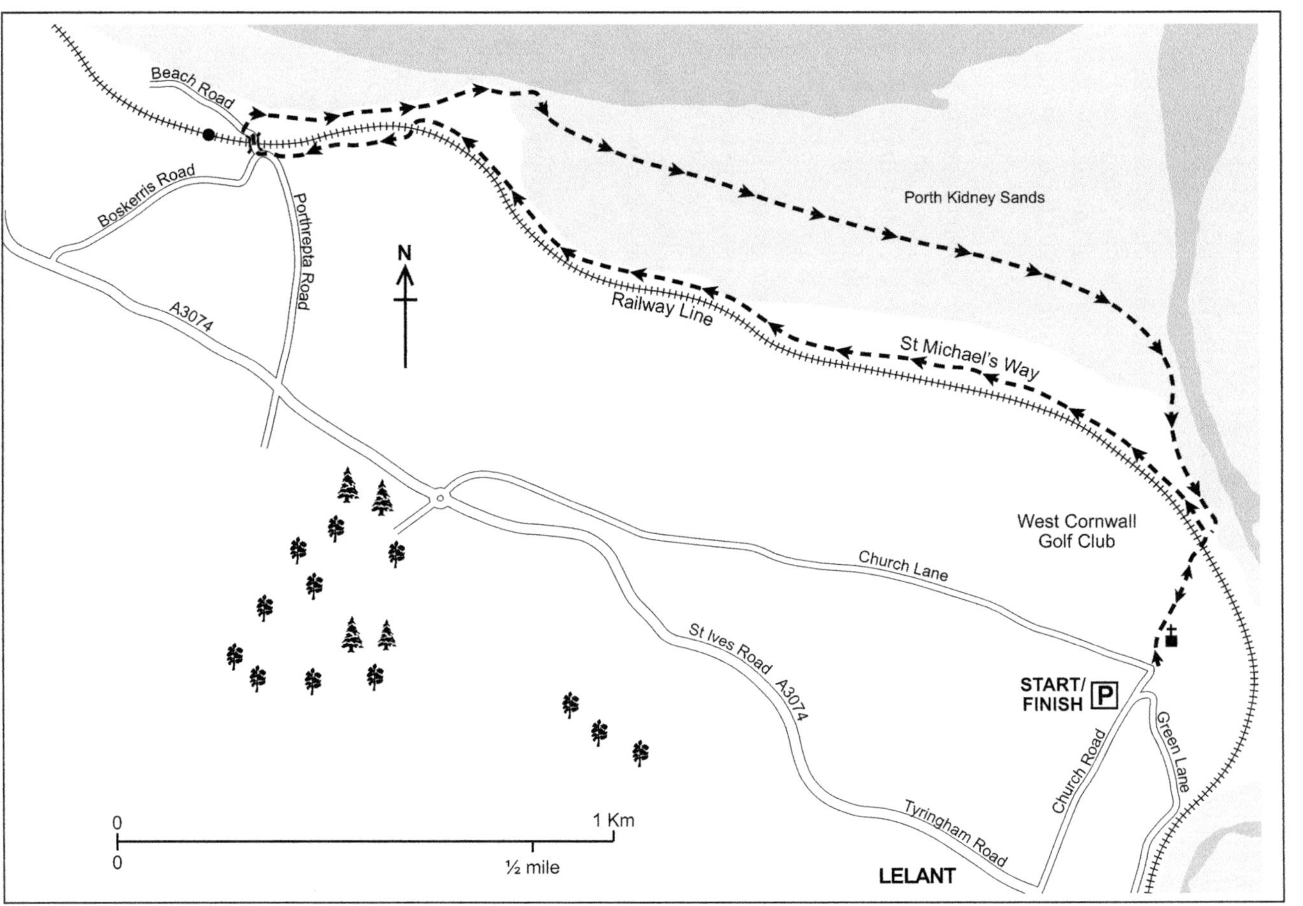

Beach Road
Boskerris Road
Porthrepta Road
A3074
Porth Kidney Sands
N
Railway Line
St Michael's Way
West Cornwall Golf Club
Church Lane
St Ives Road A3074
Church Road
Green Lane
START/FINISH P
Tyringham Road
LELANT
0
0
1 Km
½ mile

Still walking through the dunes, we meandered along paths through stumped hawthorn bushes and an even better view of the beach below us. We continued walking with the railway line on our left, while above us an aeroplane drew a crisp white line through the deep blue of the sky. Soon, we had our first glimpse of Carbis Bay ahead of us, with St Ives in the distance, and as we walked I noticed two magpies sitting in a hawthorn tree - a sign of good luck.

From here we could see the railway line hugging the coast as it made its way towards St Ives, and hear the constant, reassuring rumble of the waves on Porthkidney beach. The path moved away from the dunes and along a rocky and narrow stretch with catkins and primroses peeping from the bushes – another sign of spring. The path became steep along here while blackbirds and robins sang noisily on either side of us and the sun slanted through the fragile young branches.

The steps became steep as we grew nearer to Carbis Bay, and as the path became tarmac heading upwards into the sunshine, we saw the first three cornered leek in the hedge. At the top of the hill, we were level with the St Ives Branch railway line and saw a sign indicating Hayle 1½ miles and St Ives 1¾ miles and another sign of the St Michael's Way, a pilgrim route to Santiago and a European Cultural route. This is a 12.5 mile prehistoric route from Lelant crossing the peninsula to Marazion, avoiding the need to clamber over

Towards St Ives

submerged rocks and strong currents at Land's End. It is believed that this route was a key factor in Cornwall's rapid conversion into a Christian faith.

Coming to a junction, we continued straight ahead under some pine trees, a few chalets on our right and a wood pigeon cooing behind us. At the top of the hill we looked down at St Ives in the near distance, laid out like a sunlit painting with the sea a milky blue, and the pristine white sands of Carbis Bay before us as the tide swept out.

We crossed over the railway bridge and turned right which led us down into Carbis Bay. Barbara Hepworth and Ben Nicholson's old house is on the left as you walk along here – now a holiday home, named Chy an Kerris, if you wish to stay there.

High above Carbis Bay, on Worvas Hill, we could see a 50 foot high obelisk which was originally intended as a mausoleum to its creator, John Knill, who was the Mayor of St Ives. He was private secretary to the Earl of Buckingham, Bencher of Gray's Inn, Collector of Customs and also, apparently, a very successful smuggler. He built the town's first pier before making his fortune as inspector of Jamaican ports. It is thought that the obelisk was a useful navigational aid for Knill's smuggling activities as it can be seen for miles around.

John Knill organised a ceremony to take place on 25th July: St James the Apostle's Day, and decreed that a sum of money should be spent on food and drink. The ceremony involved ten young girls dressed in white, two widows in black and a fiddler to play the Furry Dance, and sing and dance round the town and the obelisk. This folk ceremony is still enacted here every five years on the day, making the obelisk the centre of a unique tradition.

Walking down towards Carbis Bay beach or Barrepta Cove, we noted the various holiday homes on our left and the glorious expanse of sand on our right. The name *Carbis* is from Carbis Farm which was recorded in 1391 as *Carbons* and is thought to mean *causeway*. When the St Ives railway was built, a station was created at the bottom of the Carbis Valley which was named Carbis Bay and this gradually became the name for the beach.

Coming to the road we turned right where we could see Carbis Bay station and the Carbis Bay Hotel on the left, but we followed the road round to the right and back over the railway bridge. Along here we came to a footpath sign on the right indicating Lelant Church 1¾ or St Ives 1½, so we followed the path down some sandy steps and then turned right, eastwards, back along the South West coast path, parallel to the beach.

Looking out over St Ives Bay we were struck by the different shades of the sea – streaks of dark blue, patches of royal blue and milky blue-green areas, edged by a delicate lacing of waves. A lone fishing boat chugged back into harbour, trailing a stream of noisy gulls, and on the beach was a single walker, with three dogs barking excitedly as they scampered along the sand.

Climbing up some steps and down the other side, we found a steep cliff face covered in bracken on our right and relaxed in the warmth of the sun. Rounding the headland of Carrack Gladden, we noted a large wooden house above on our right and below that a path leading down to the beach. If the tide is in, take the footpath sign on the right which will take you to meet the path we walked in on.

As the tide was out, we climbed down some steep steps, over rocks until we reached Porthkidney beach, where a group of people were playing football. Apart from them, we were the only people on this huge expanse of sand. "I'm tempted to take my boots off and walk in bare feet," I said to Ursula. "I love the feeling of and between my toes." But then a brisk breeze sped along the sand, and I decided against it.

We walked back towards Lelant, jumping over pools in the ridged sand, while Moll raced up and down like a puppy, instead of the 84 year old that she is (in dog years). There are various paths on the right that lead through the dunes and back onto the footpath that we walked in on, but we opted to continue as far as we could, then carry round the corner of the beach, where the river Hayle flows incredibly fast into the sea – this is very dangerous so please don't try and cross it either on foot or afloat.

Continuing round, southward now, we walked with the river on our left while Moll explored several interesting looking caves. Due to the bad weather of recent winters, a certain amount of coastal erosion has occurred, leaving the debris of fallen cliffs on the beach, so don't get too near the base of the cliffs. Soon we came to a public footpath sign leading up a flight of very steep steps past a house named Ferryman's Rest on the right and we walked uphill with the church tower ahead of us. We passed a sign for West Cornwall Golf Club, and soon we reached the church and the layby where we'd parked the car.

"Shall we see the house where Rosamunde Pilcher spent her childhood?" asked Ursula, who is an expert in these matters. "Yes please," I said, so we walked back the way we had driven, then turned first left, opposite Chygwidden Cottage. Following the road round to the right, past the turning to Dynamite Quay, we continued along a narrow road with tall firs on the right, as well as bamboos and a huge palm tree. As a pigeon cooed on the distance, we came to a house named Trengilly with a gate and the following old sign on it, which made us laugh: *Any person who omits to shut and fasten this gate is liable to a penalty not exceeding forty shillings.*

At the bottom of the hill the road flattens, and on the right we saw several large houses, set back from the road fronted by large gardens. Ursula pointed to the last house but one. "That's it," she said. "That's where Rosamunde Pilcher spent much of her childhood." We stood and gazed at the large, proud house with wonderful views. "What an amazing place for children to grow up in," I said. "That big garden to get lost and explore in. A place for the imagination to take root."

Further along is the old station which is now a chalet style fronted house named, appropriately, The Old Station House and past here we turned right, leaving Lelant Station behind us. We climbed up the hill noticing a small wooded area named Anne's Wood, which was given to the Woodland Trust in memory of Anne Rostron. This stands on the site of a 19th century clay works which were used to make firebricks for lining furnaces in South Wales. This looks like a lovely, much used adventure playground for children with lots of beech, sycamore, oak and ash trees to climb.

At the top of this hill (Station Road) is the Badger Inn and on the corner of The Old Bakery, we turned right down Church Road following signs to St Uny Church and the Golf Links. There are some beautiful old houses along here which make the walk all the more worthwhile, and I love knowing that this was one of Rosamunde Pilcher's favourite walks: that we really were walking in her footsteps.

ST IVES

An artist's haven and the scene of many of Rosamunde Pilcher films

St Ives was called Porthkerris in some of Rosamunde Pilcher's books, and has been used in many of the Pilcher films. In *The Lights Games*, the Sliding Tackle pub is the St Ives Arts Club, and Gallery Amber is Westcott's Gallery, both in Westcott's Quay.

St Ives is mentioned as Porthkerris and Joss is beaten up in front of the Sloop Inn in *Stormy Encounters.* In this film, Rosamunde Pilcher herself appears in this scene (as Hitchcock did in his films), where Rebecca stands in front of the Porthkerris Gallery – this is in fact the Wills Lane Gallery in Back Street.

In *The Long Road to Happiness*, the funeral took place at Barnoon Cemetery, near the Tate Gallery, overlooking Porthmeor Beach.

Stella and her husband Peter end up on Smeaton's Pier in *The Secret of the White Dove.* And *In the Middle of a Life*, Wharf Road was the venue for the meeting between Richard, Ella, Michael and Carol, with Smeaton's Pier as a backdrop. High above St Ives is a private, white house that was Betty's home, from where you can see St Ives Island with St Nicholas's Chapel and Porthmeor Beach.

On arrival at St Ives, you will see why the light, the way the houses cluster around the harbour and the little island, has attracted many well known painters, sculptors and ceramicists such as JMW Turner and Henry Moore for centuries.

There is also the world-famous Tate Gallery, which opened in 1993 in recognition of the international importance of art in Cornwall and St. Ives in particular. Here you can see hundreds of works produced by the St. Ives

School from the late 1800s through to the 21st century, and the gallery has become so popular that it has recently expanded.

Another place worth visiting is the Barbara Hepworth Museum and Sculpture Garden, showing some of her most famous bronze and limestone works. Towards the top of the town is the Bernard Leach Pottery, first established in 1920, that is now a working museum.

There are numerous other galleries and exhibitions that attract famous artists all year round, and four fabulous beaches – Porthmeor, Porthgwidden, Harbour beach and Porthminster. Together with plenty of shops, pavement cafes, restaurants and old pubs, you won't be short of entertainment in St Ives.

What you need to know	
Distance	3 miles approximately
Allow	3 hours including refreshment stop and look at shops
Suggested Map	OS Explorer 102 Land's End, Penzance & St Ives
Starting point	St Erth station. Grid ref: SW 541 357
Terrain	Mostly flat, steep hill up to Carbis Bay
Nearest refreshments	Plenty in St Ives
Public transport	Train from St Erth to St Ives; plenty of buses, check local Tourist Information
Of interest	Tate Gallery, Barbara Hepworth Museum, Knills Monument, 4 beaches
Facilities	Plenty in St Ives

The Walk

One windy day in November, Viv, MollieDog and I headed off to St Erth to catch the train to St Ives. Despite the many years I have lived in Cornwall, I'd never taken this train ride though I have often walked the coastal path beside it, so I knew how beautiful it was. I decided it was time I experienced this magical ride.

The trains were every half hour to St Ives (check for timings) and the trip took ten minutes, with some of the loveliest views I have ever seen from a train window. Leaving St Erth, the next stop was Lelant Saltings with the flat marshes, so beloved of bird watchers, spread out before us. Further on, we looked out over St Ives Bay and saw Godrevy lighthouse in the far distance, the miles of sand that lead down to Hayle, then Porth Kidney Sands and round to Carbis Bay, before we arrived at St Ives.

The train ride really is well worth doing, and spares the hassle of driving round St Ives searching for a parking space. And at a cost of £4 return (dogs go free), we felt this was good value. There's also the Branch Line tea room at St Erth which we weren't able to sample as we had to get our train, but it looked promising.

At St Ives station, we followed the signs to the beaches, down a flight of steps. This led us to Porthminster, where the tide was out so we were able to enjoy the wide expanse of golden sand along with other dog walkers. As we looked towards the sea, we noticed what we thought were large dogs playing in the surf – it turned out they were seals! These mammals look cute, but they are very shy and can bite, so please don't go near them. We watched, entranced, for some minutes, before walking north west round the rocks until we reached the Harbour beach, then West Pier and the Lifeboat Station.

St Ives at low tide

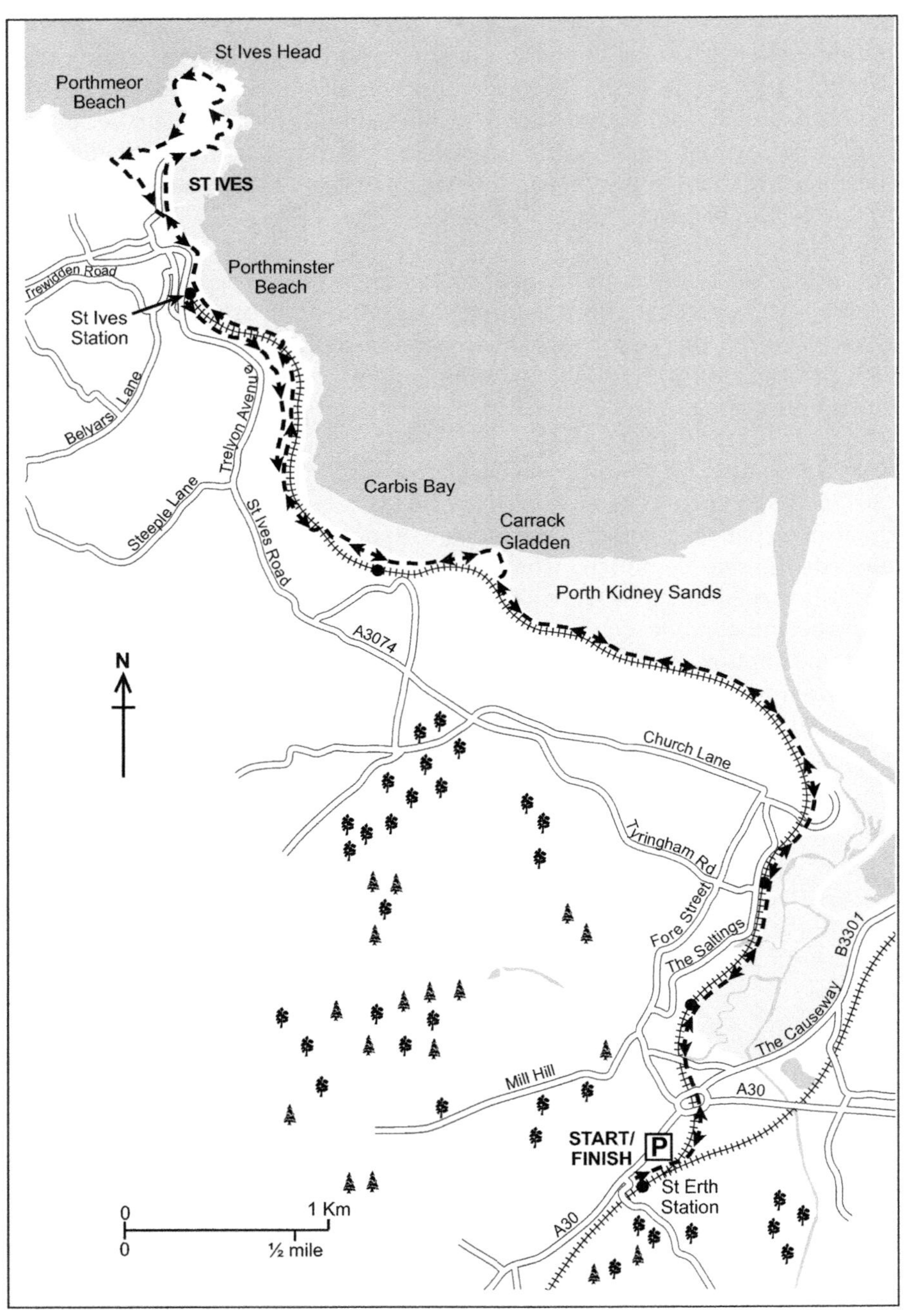

St Ives Head
Porthmeor Beach
ST IVES
Trewidden Road
St Ives Station
Porthminster Beach
Belyars Lane
Steeple Lane
Trelyon Avenue
St Ives Road
Carbis Bay
Carrack Gladden
Porth Kidney Sands
A3074
N
Church Lane
Tyringham Rd
Fore Street
The Saltings
The Causeway
B3301
Mill Hill
A30
START/ FINISH
P
St Erth Station
A30
0
1 Km
0
½ mile

The Sloop Inn

We walked, due north, along by the shops so we could see Whistlefish Gallery, on the junction of Wharf Road and Back Lane, as filmed in *Totally Unexpected*, where Hannah drops her shopping bag and Eric helps her collect everything. Filming also took place at the lifeboat station and the Sloop Inn, which is very near the gallery. This pub is thought to date back to around 1312 AD and as it is right on the harbour front, is popular with locals, fishermen, artists and visitors alike. It's only a stone's throw from all the shops, galleries and the famous Tate Gallery.

From the Sloop, we walked eastwards along the Wharf (Harbour front) to Smeaton's Pier and Bamaluz beach, from where boat trips leave, then wandered northwards round the back streets, past Downalong Cottage, then St Ives Museum, which is full of memorabilia and artefacts that reflect St Ives's long and varied history of fishing, boatbuilding, art and agriculture. After the museum, we reached Wheal Dream car park and found a path on our right that led round to Porthgwidden Beach.

This beach was almost deserted, so we enjoyed another walk on the fine sands before climbing up and walking round the headland, known as The Island, and up to the St Ives Lookout Station. There was a little shop here selling second hand books as well as cards and notebooks, so we bought some of these before checking out St Nicholas's Chapel. He was the patron saint of sailors, as well as children, but curiously there is no record of when this chapel was built. However, there has been a chapel here since 1434, a time when Irish missionaries made their pilgrimage to Rome via St Ives.

At one time, customs officers used this building to look out for smugglers, and vice versa. In the 19th century, the chapel was used as a storeroom for the nearby gun battery (the present coastguard lookout). Threatened with demolition in 1904, the chapel was saved by the town and restored in 1911 to commemorate the Coronation of King George V. It was restored again in 1971 and is still used for weekly services.

From here we walked westwards, down the other side of The Island towards Porthmeor Beach. This is the largest beach in St Ives, where you can take lessons at the St Ives Surf School, and it is also very close to the Tate Gallery and many of the other artists' studios and galleries. But we enjoyed another walk along the beach, then retreated to the Porthmeor Cafe for a coffee, or hot chocolate in Viv's case.

This cafe is very popular in all seasons, and welcomes those of us with dogs. At the far end of the cafe, towards the toilets, we found a series of cosy outdoor covered booths with heaters and even blankets to keep you warm during inclement weather. We found the service prompt and cheerful, the drinks were good and the food looked delicious - well worth a try next time we visit.

Leaving the cafe we turned south (left) to walk back through town, along the Digey, which led us back to Fore Street and the harbour. At the far end of Fore Street we came across the lovely old shop front of Leddra the chemist, as filmed in *Totally Unexpected*.

From here we turned left down Lifeboat Hill, back to the lifeboat station and West Pier, where we turned right and noted the lovely ridged patterns of sand on the beach as the tide came in.

Past Porthminster Gallery, then up the hill, we followed signs to the St Ives Branch Line. Instead of walking up to the station, via the flight of steps on our right (which we had walked down on arrival), we continued along the path towards Carbis Bay, round the back of Porthminster Beach.

The path leads steadily uphill along a tarmac path through a coppiced area, with the railway on our left which runs parallel to the coast. After an old quarry on our right, we looked back over the beautiful expanse of Porthminster Beach and the Harbour behind and thought how lucky we are to live here.

At the top of this hill we came to a junction and carried straight on, following a yellow waymark sign along the higher footpath route through the outskirts of St Ives, then came to a road and continued ahead. Further along, we passed the Baulking House, a Grade II listed building, probably built in the early 19th century. This was a huer's lookout from where they would look out for pilchard shoals and shout down (as in hue and cry) to the fishermen.

Along a quiet area with trees on either side, past Treloyan Manor Hotel up in the trees on our right, we followed the footpath signs through a residential area along a rough tarmac road. From now on our way was veering eastwards. We came to a junction with several footpaths, including one to Knills Monument, a 50-foot-high granite obelisk that towers over St Ives and dates back over two centuries. This structure was the last work of the renowned architect John Wood the Younger of Batheaston, designer of the Royal Crescent in Bath, and was built in 1782 as a mausoleum and memorial for a mayor of St. Ives, John Knill.

However, we took the turning ahead to St Michael's Way and Lelant 2.5 miles which led downhill to Carbis Bay and Barrepta beach spread out before us.

We crossed over the railway line via a bridge, then continued to the outskirts of the Carbis Bay Hotel where the path was diverted through the grounds owing to building works. Reaching the car park, we turned right up the hill, under a viaduct and up a steep hill which led round to the left, past the hotel apartments, with a stream on our left. Coming to the end of the cottages, we crossed over a little footbridge on our left over the stream, and reached a wooded path, looking down through the viaduct arches to the beach.

This path led to a collection of new apartments, and further on, the Carbis Bay station car park. We'd just missed a train, but the next one came along in 15 minutes, and took us back to St Erth – a truly lovely afternoon, and one that I'm sure Rosamunde Pilcher herself would have enjoyed on many an occasion.

TREEN, PORTHCURNO AND THE MINACK THEATRE

Minack means 'rocky place' in Cornish and when you visit this unique open air theatre, built into the cliffs, you will see why. This is surely one of the most beautiful open air theatres in the world and is open from May to October, showing a wide variety of dramas, musicals and opera.

Over 80,000 people come to see performances at the Minack every year, and more than 150,000 visitors come to look round during the day, to experience this unique stage which still carries the vision of its extraordinary founder, Rowena Cade.

Minack Theatre

Such a dramatic backdrop just begs to be filmed, and so the Minack Theatre has featured in *Light Games, Time of Knowledge*, when Sarah Brightman sang *Scarborough Fair*, and in *Argentine Tango*, Valentina tries to teach Jack the tango at the Minack. Also, Mona and Stephan take the boat to the Minack Theatre in *Summer of Awakening*.

In the book, *The World of Rosamunde Pilcher*, there is a colour plate of Laura Knight's painting, *At the Edge of the Cliff* and underneath a quote about the painting from *The Shell Seekers:* "Laura Knight. What a particular beauty that is ... That was done at Porthcurno."

What you need to know	
Distance	**3.5 miles**
Allow	**2 hours not including visit to beach, theatre, museum or refreshments**
Suggested Map	**OS Explorer 102 Land's End, Penzance & St Ives**
Starting point	**Treen campsite Grid ref: SW 394 229**
Terrain	**Few steep hills**
Nearest refreshments	**Treen cafe, Logan Rock pub, Minack Theatre cafe, Telegraph Museum cafe at Porthcurno**
Public transport	**Atlantic Coaster A1 from Penzance to bus shelter near Treen, then 5 minute walk**
Of interest	**Penberth Plants http://www.penberthplants.co.uk, Minack Theatre, Porthcurno Telegraph Museum and shop, Porthcurno beach, Logan Rock**
Facilities	**Treen campsite, Porthcurno**

The Walk

One Sunday morning early in June, Steve, MollieDog and I drove down to Penzance, and from there we continued along the A30 and followed signs to Land's End. We drove through the village of Drift, then came to Catchall (the road sign almost obscured by overgrown hedgerows) and turned left along the B3283 signed to St Buryan. A few miles further on, we turned left to Treen, past the 16th century Logan Rock pub and continued round to the left, past

Treen Hill
St Buryan Hill
B3315
N
TREEN
START/ FINISH
P
PORTHCURNO
Telegraph Museum
The Valley
Penberth Cove
Coast Path
Minack Theatre
Minack Point
Teryn Dynas Fort
Cripp's Cove
0
0
1 Km
½ mile

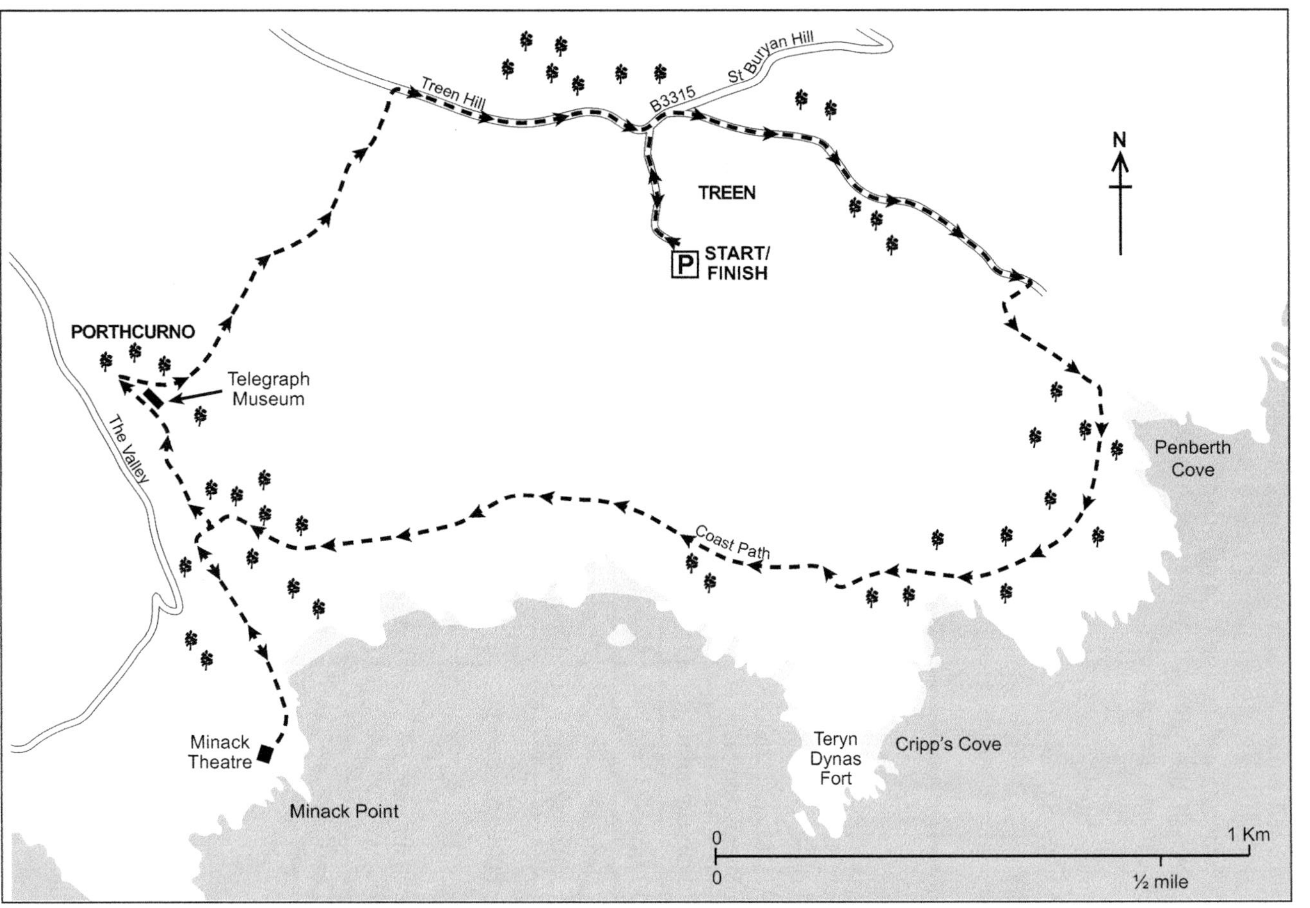

70

the Treen cafe to park in the campsite car park which at the time of walking was £2 per day. There are public toilets here at a cost of 20p.

From the car park we headed back the way we'd driven in, past an old phone box that now houses a defibrillator, then past Treen Farm on the right and the Logan Rock pub on our left, looking very colourful with many hanging baskets brimming with riotous summer colour and a large outdoor seating area. At the junction of the main road, we turned right and, opposite a flower and vegetable stall, turned first right again signed Penberth ¾ mile.

We walked down a quiet narrow lane with high hedges crammed full of pink campion, deep yellow buttercups, cow parsley and the last faded bluebells, while above us blackbirds sang loudly on this breezy morning. Sycamore trees lined the lane, their leaves rustling in the wind, while the fading blackthorn blossom had turned a rusty colour.

Walking downhill, we came to a beautiful sheltered little valley with clusters of bamboos growing in among various cottages, before arriving at an old mill and Penberth Gardens. These prize winning gardens cover five acres of rocky garden with tumbling stream bog plants, camellias, azaleas and other shrubs among massive natural boulders.

Many of these plants, originally from South Africa and bred from seed, grow naturally here so that now around 9,000 plant species from the Cape Floral Kingdom flourish, so it is well worth a visit. Unfortunately the gardens were shut on the day we walked, as the owners were away at a horticultural show, but we noticed many different types of bamboo and dracaena as well as the biggest, blowsiest red poppies I've ever seen.

Further on we saw an exuberant rhododendron in the richest red, and laughed at a sign saying *Please Drive Slowly, Cats Crossing*, though we didn't see any. Instead the hedges boasted ragged robin, the first honeysuckle and three cornered leek; a few squashed garlic.

We continued past a thatched cottage with a dovecot at the end and then reached the tiny, picturesque Penberth Cove. It is still used for fishing, so visitors are asked to cross the stream using the stepping stones provided, rather than clogging up the slipway. The boats are hauled up the slip (or cauance as it is known locally) by an electric winch, rather than the spectacular capstan which can be seen in the centre of the cove, and has been restored by the National Trust. Penberth Cove was once part of the pilchard fishing industry, though today the local fishermen make their living fishing for lobster, mackerel and crab. There used to be a cut flower business here, with the flowers sent to London via train from Penzance.

Having crossed the stream via the stepping stones, we took the coastal footpath westward next to the wooden winch house on the right of the cove. This path is quite steep and rocky, so be careful and watch where you're walking. We saw the first foxgloves along here and looked back several times to admire the cove – the cottage nearest to the sea has a bouquet of colourful fishing floats outside it, like giant gob stoppers, and we were able to admire the superb geology of this coastline. After quite a long steep climb, finally we reached the top and were rewarded with the most incredible views along the coastline past Coffin Rock to Merthen Point behind us to the East.

Penberth Cove

From here you can also see the famous headland of Logan Rock to the south-west, on the left. The 80 ton stone sadly lost a lot of its rocking balance when it was dislodged by a group of young naval officers in 1824. Prior to this it could be rocked using a tiny bit of pressure.

It's possible to see the Scillonian ferry on its way to the Isles of Scilly from this area of the coastpath if you get the timing right. Today we saw a fishing boat and a few yachts, and enjoyed an army of foxgloves, lining the way like proud purple soldiers. This path meanders inland, through a few wrought iron gates, and over a stream where Moll had a drink. The path splits to go back to Treen on the right, but we continued along the coastal footpath.

As we walked, we could see the Minack Theatre in the distance, before coming to a junction where we turned left on a slight detour to see the remains of Treryn Dinas, an Iron Age Hill fort on the headland of Logan Rock.

This site, also called Treen Castle, was protected by sheer cliffs to three sides while the landward side was heavily defended. These defences consist of three sets of large ramparts and ditches, the first, and largest of which measured nearly 20ft (6.5m) high and 800ft (250m) long. The second rampart is smaller and located a couple of hundred feet (80m) closer to the promontory. The third line of defences is a rampart and ditch running across the 'saddle' of the headland where it narrows considerably.

According to local folklore, Treen Castle was the work of the giant Dan Dynas, and bad luck would befall anyone who removed any of the rocks. However, as most of the rock was taken away, the superstition obviously didn't last long. As cremated bone has been found here, it's thought that Treryn Dinas may have been used for religious or ceremonial purposes rather than as a settlement.

Having explored the headland, we walked back to the footpath and turned left, across common land, from where we could see the milky turquoise seas off Porthcurno Beach, and a closer view of the Minack Theatre built into the cliffs ahead. Today some lights illuminated the stage, so presumably they were rehearsing the lighting cues. Ponies grazed along here, and all kinds of granite boulders are perched along the cliffs at precarious angles, as well as scattered along the footpath.

We came to a junction where the public bridleway led straight on, but we followed the coastal footpath to the left, though it seems that both routes end up at Porthcurno.

Further on, we came to another junction and took the path leading straight ahead, but you could take the left hand path which is very steep and leads down to Pedn Vounder beach, popular with nudists. At very low spring tides, it is possible to walk from here to Porthcurno, but the beach consists of sand bars meaning that some parts of the beach flood faster than others, so it is easy to be caught by the tide.

The inner path we took was overgrown, and lined with vetch, dandelion and hawthorn trees, while butterflies fluttered in and out of the tall hedges. Soon we headed downhill along a rocky path shaded by sycamore trees that ends up on the path that leads up to the village to the right and down to the beach on the left. Do take time to enjoy this wonderful beach that was recommended in the Good Beach Guide 2015. Porthcurno has very fine soft white sand and the sea really does look turquoise in the sun. The high cliffs provide plenty of shelter, making it a perfect family beach, with a stream that flows down one side. Dogs are banned from 8am-7pm in summer months and there is lifeguard cover in the summer – check the website for exact details.

From the beach, it's a short steep walk up the hill to visit the Minack Theatre which was devised by Rowena Cade, who lived at Minack House and decided that the cliffs below would be the perfect place for a theatre. Over the winter of 1931 she and her gardener, Billy Rawlings, moved huge amounts of earth and granite boulders to create the lower terraces of the theatre. Although the cliffs are made of granite, most of the theatre is made from concrete mixed with local beach sand, and Rowena carried many tons of sand from the beach to the theatre, where the concrete was used for seats, steps, walkways and pillars. The names of plays or performance were carved into the wet concrete of many of the seats, making the theatre even more personalised and special.

A few years before, in 1929, the local drama club had put on an open air performance of *A Midsummer Night's Dream* in a field about a mile inland

Porthcurno

View from the Minack

from the Minack. It was such a triumph that the players wanted to find another venue to perform *The Tempest*. Rowena's theatre was just the right place, and *The Tempest* was an even bigger success, getting a good review in *The Times*.

Over the years, Rowena and her gardeners made a lot of improvements, creating what has become the stage structures of today. The first dressing rooms were not built until 1954, and the current dressing rooms were built on the same site in 2011, but today even the biggest companies have enough facilities and storage space for equipment at the Minack.

After visiting the theatre, instead of going to the cafe there, we decided to try the Telegraph Museum cafe, so we walked down to the Telegraph Museum which can be reached via the car park at Porthcurno. Steve knows much more about the history of Porthcurno so I shall hand over to him, "In the 19th century, many transatlantic submarine telegraph cables came ashore at Porthcurno," he said. "The first was landed in 1870 as part of an early international link between the UK and India, which was then a British colony."

"Why choose Porthurno?" I wondered.

"Because Falmouth was a very busy port and the cables could easily have been damaged by ships' anchors," he replied. "In 1872 the Eastern Telegraph Company (ETC) was formed and took over operation of the cables and built a concrete cable office up the valley in Porthcurno. This was where the cable shore ends were connected to their respective landlines, and you can still see the hut at the top of the beach – it's a listed building."

It appears that the cable operations expanded through the late 19th and early 20th centuries and in 1928 merged with Marconi's Wireless Telegraph Company Ltd to form Imperial and International Communications Ltd – renamed Cable and Wireless Limited in 1934 and later, Cable and Wireless Worldwide.

"In between the wars, up to 14 cables were operated, and for a time this was the biggest submarine cable station in the world, able to receive and transmit up to two million words a day," he added.

"Many apprentices were trained in telepathy at Porthcurno, then in 1950 Cable and Wireless opened an engineering course at Porthcurno providing courses in telecommunications. The cable office closed in 1970, exactly 100 years after the first cable was landed but the college stayed open until 1993. Since then the award winning Porthcurno Telegraph Museum opened, meaning that this extraordinary part of telecommunications history can be shared with visitors."

By this time we were walking up the path to the right of the car park, towards the Telegraph Museum. "Would you believe it?" cried Steve. "Despite this area being the founder of telecommunications, I've got no signal on my phone!" Amazing how modern technology is confounded by nature, although rather smugly I found that I did have a signal on my older, far more inferior phone.

Walking uphill past an Anderson Shelter, we came to the Museum which also has a well stocked shop with plenty of books and other information. We headed for the cafe and found some picnic tables and chairs outside, and enjoyed a cup of coffee and a piece of fruit cake with Moll while looking out over the tennis courts below, and the steps to the theatre and beach in the distance.

Suitably refreshed, and leaving the museum behind us, we walked uphill and inland along the drive, adjacent to the bunker entrance, past a large greenhouse on the left, behind a large wall, and came to a sharp right hand turn which led along a steep grassy path which had recently been mown. At the top, where it opened out, was another mown path to the left which leads back to a signpost indicating how far Porthcurno is from e.g. Rio de Janiero 5,550 miles and Newfoundland 2,000 miles.

We continued straight on, and coming to a field, walked down the middle of a crop of barley, towards Tredrennen Farm ahead of us. Heading over a stile by a faded waymark sign, we continued through another field (of potatoes this time), until we came to Tredrennen Barn and then the farm behind it.

Looking at the OS map, there is a public footpaths to the right, east of the farm leading back to Treen, but on the day we walked, some of the access had been blocked by new fencing, so we were forced to abandon the rural route. If following in our footsteps, from the farm we walked straight ahead northwards along the drive until we came to the main road where we turned right, walked along for about five minutes and then turned right again back into Treen. We walked uphill, past the pub and then continued back to the car park, marvelling at all that we'd seen in just a few hours of walking.

There is so much to delight any fans of Rosamunde Pilcher on this walk – from the incredible turquoise seas and beach of Porthcurno to the unique Minack Theatre perched on the edge of the cliffs. Add in the extraordinary history of communications, and there is something for everyone!

MOUSEHOLE TO LAMORNA COVE

Lamorna Cove provided some of the breathtaking Cornish scenery for the filming of four of Rosamunde Pilcher's stories – *The Empty House, Another View, Voices In Summer* and *Snow In April* – screened by Frankfurter Filmproduktion. Lamorna also featured in the British production of *The Shell Seekers,* starring Vanessa Redgrave.

Apart from the natural beauty of this cove, Lamorna is perhaps best known for the Post-Impressionist artists who stayed here early on in the 20th century. Samuel Birch even took his name from the place, calling himself Lamorna Birch, and after his move here, many other of the Newlyn School of artists joined him.

Lamorna Cove

Some of these artists included Laura Knight, and her husband, Harold Knight, Alfred Munnings and Augustus John. Writers, potters, artists and craftspeople have long been drawn here and some of the better known writers are John Le Carre and Derek Tangye. There are still many writers, artists and potters who live near here and much of their work can be seen at Lamorna Pottery, and shops in Mousehole and Penzance.

What you need to know	
Distance	5 miles
Allow	4 hours including several refreshment stops
Suggested Map	OS Explorer 102 Land's End, Penzance & St Ives
Starting point	Pier car park. Grid ref: SW 470 263
Terrain	Steep and rough in parts
Nearest refreshments	Plenty in Mousehole and Lamorna
Public transport	346 and M6 buses from Penzance
Of interest	Mousehole village; Carn Du headland, Lamorna Cove, Lamorna Wink, panoramic views of Mount's Bay and St Michael's Mount
Facilities	Mousehole, Lamorna

The Walk

One sunny Tuesday in mid October Fiona, MollieDog and I drove through Penzance, then Newlyn, and parked in a layby on the outskirts of Mousehole, though parking is also available on North Pier and other car parks in Mousehole. From here we wandered southwards along the harbour front, enjoying the autumn sun as many others were doing, playing on the beaches as the tide was out.

Mousehole was the major port in Mount's Bay in mediaeval times, and in the 14th century, its fishing fleet was much larger than Penzance or Newlyn. The name Mousehole (pronounced Mouzel) is thought to have come from a cave known as The Mousehole which was used by smugglers. If you climb over rocks to the west you will see the cave with a completely round entrance, like a mouse hole.

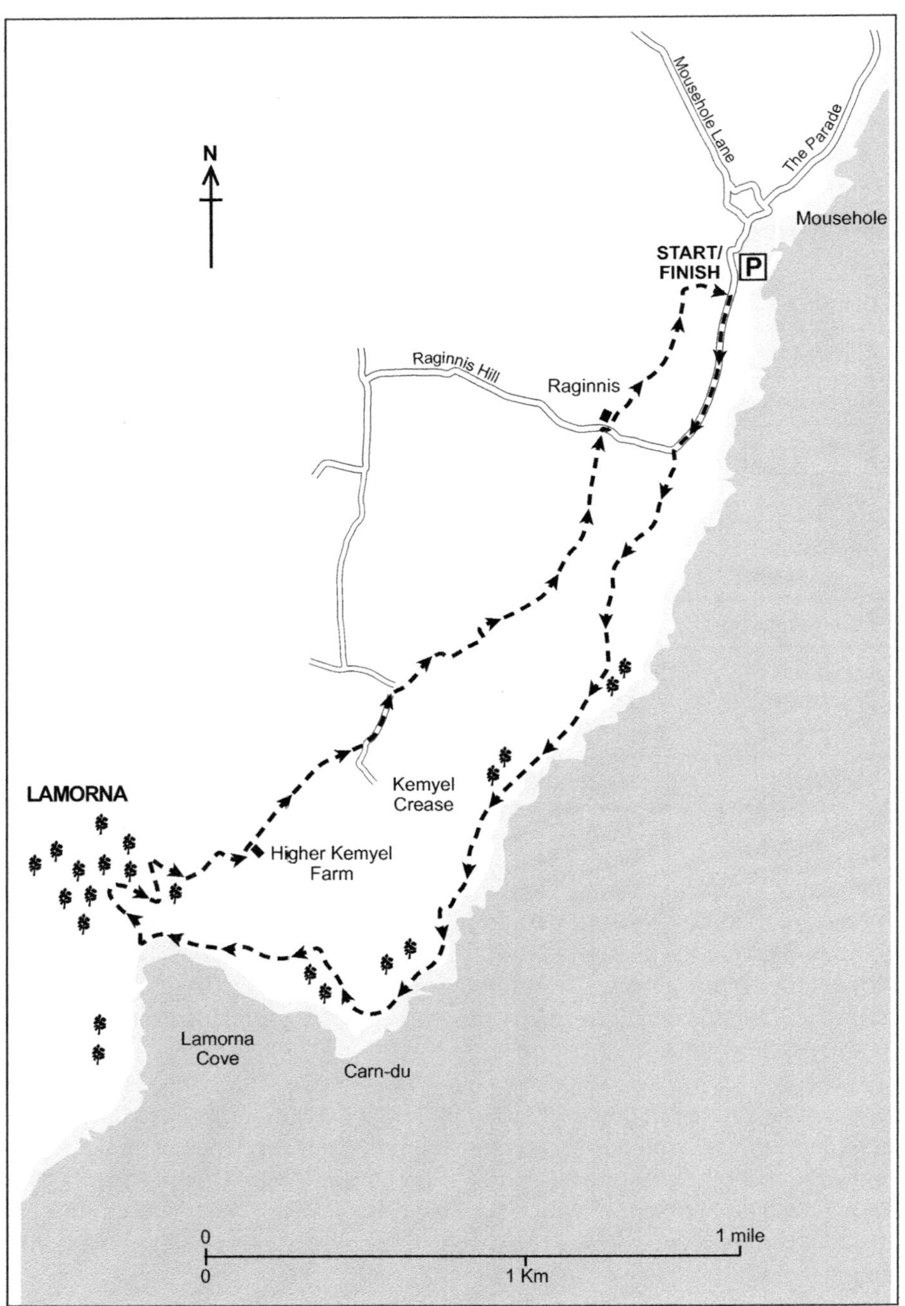

N
Mousehole Lane
The Parade
Mousehole
START/
FINISH
P
Raginnis Hill
Raginnis
Kemyel
Crease
LAMORNA
Higher Kemyel
Farm
Lamorna
Cove
Carn-du
0
0
1 mile
1 Km

We passed the Ship Inn and continued until we reached Keigwin Place, where we turned left following the coastpath sign and then reached a T-junction opposite Little Keigwin. The building on the right is Keigwin House, which dates from the 14th century and is the oldest building in the town.

In 1595, during the Anglo-Spanish War, five Spanish ships moored just outside Mousehole carrying several hundred men. The Spaniards raped the women, killed everyone they found, looted the town and burnt everything to the ground. The only house that remained is Keigwin House which was formerly the Keigwin Arms and probably remained because it was the only stone building.

On the left is a plaque dedicated to Dolly Pentreath, one of the last people to speak the Cornish language. It's fascinating to wander around these old back streets, imagining how life was hundreds of years ago.

We crossed through the car park, to the left of the Rowing Club, pausing to take photographs in the soft sunlight, and followed a narrow path to reach a lane in front of Glas Mor. Here we turned left, round a sharp bend and walked uphill to a sign for Merlin Place. Unsure of the route, we found another coast path sign and continued southwards up the steep Raginnis Hill.

This hill is very steep and long, but we stopped to look back at the fabulous views over Mounts Bay where the water seemed mirror calm, and St Michael's Mount rose from the glassy sea like a magical castle. The Mousehole Bird Hospital and Sanctuary was founded along here by two sisters in 1928. In 1967 the Torrey Canyon ship was wrecked, near Land's End, resulting in a horrific oil spill that killed thousands of seabirds. Thankfully Mousehole Bird Sanctuary was able to treat over 8,000 birds and the Sanctuary is now a registered charity, relying on voluntary contributions. Visitors are welcome and it is free.

The road flattened out and where it took a right angle turn to the west we left it by a coastal footpath sign indicating Lamorna 2 miles. The stony track passed Porth Enys House and became narrow, with high hedges on either side, and – mysteriously – we saw an abandoned buggy parked in the middle of the path. We searched for a child and/or parent, finding none but to our relief, further along we came across a young German mother and little boy. "It was too hard pushing the buggy so we just left it," she said with a broad smile. Her son gave a gappy grin and was fascinated by Mollie who submitted to his pats with a good grace.

The sun grew hotter as we walked along the coastal path for about a mile due south, sometimes very steep up and down, until we reached the wooded area of Kemyel Crease Nature Reserve. Not many conifers grow along the coast but Monterey Pine and Cypress trees were planted here in Victorian times as windbreaks when bulbs and potatoes were grown in tiny terraced fields called quillets.

We continued through the woodland to find a reserve sign and walked through a gap in the wall to a waymark sign at the bottom of some steep steps. Climbing up to another waymark at the top, we had panoramic views across the bay to Tater Du lighthouse which was built in 1965 after eleven lives were lost when a Spanish coaster capsized. There is a small path leading onto Carn Du headland but it's not advisable to take this when it's wet or windy. Today was perfect: in fact we met a couple enjoying a picnic there.

We descended the steep, winding path now heading westwards, and clambered over huge lumps of granite down towards Lamorna, enjoying the sunlight sparkling on the water, the jagged lumps of rock that form the cliffs, and the frothy waves that constantly pound against the granite in a never ending quest to break it down.

As we neared the cove, we noted how quiet it was - only the odd cry of a seagull and the distant drone of a hedgecutter. We followed the path along a garden wall to reach a junction of paths and continued ahead, walking by a footbridge over a stream, past several cottages and a large patch of gunnera before we finally arrived at Lamorna quay.

In the 1800s a large London stonemasonry company was searching for accessible granite quarry sites and was delighted to find Lamorna Cove. The quarry on the eastern side of the cove opened in 1849 and several others nearby followed, where granite was blasted and chipped into shape by hand. The blocks were exported by boat from Lamorna using a two tier metal pier, with the result that Lamorna granite has been used in Wolf Rock and Longships lighthouses, many parts of London such as New Scotland Yard and the Embankment, and Dover Admiralty Pier. The current owner has not been able to maintain the pier, which was almost destroyed by the huge storms of 2014 and 2018, so the cove came up for sale in June 2018; this would be an ideal opportunity to save a beautiful part of Cornish heritage.

If you wish to explore Lamorna or go to the Wink pub, take the narrow road inland and uphill on the right. However, we decided to visit the Lamorna Cove

Cafe and sat outside inhaling the ozone tang in the air (they do allow dogs inside, but it was a shame to waste the weather). There is parking on the quay but not many spaces. After sharing a very good pistachio cake, we retraced our route until we reached the junction of paths near some houses (to return the way we'd come we would have gone straight on). We took the left fork inland, noting the massive quarry looming overhead. "Isn't the smell of autumn wonderful?" said Fiona as we walked eastwoods uphill, crunching on the crisp leaves in this wooded valley.

The steep path zig zags around the back of this huge granite works – "makes you realise how much industry came out of here," I said – before the path flattens out and we came to a public footpath sign in front of Higher Kemyel Farm. This led to a track going north east past some holiday cottages before reaching a stone stile on our right which led into a field with the most stunning views over Mount's Bay. In in the distance, the Lizard peninsula sneaked out into the sea like a lazy dragon.

Following a waymark sign next to a gate, we walked through a field slightly to the left, over another stile next to a barn and into the next field at Kemyel Point where we came to another cluster of barns and Kemyel Crease farmhouse. The late afternoon sun was beginning to be obscured by clouds, so we put on our jumpers as the shadows lengthened and the sea turned a darker blue.

Shortly after Kemyel Crease farm, we saw a public footpath sign on our right which led over another stile into a grassy field, round to the left and over another stile, down a narrow path with bracken and overhanging branches and a stream running alongside. All we could hear were a few bumble bees buzzing in the warm air, a rook in the far distance, and the low hum of a small aeroplane.

Walking through the muddy farmyard, we followed the path round the back of the buildings and into a field with a standing stone. The path led over several stiles into a succession of fields, many of which had standing stones, until we came to Raginnis Farm. Leaving the Raginnis buildings on our left, we could see Paul church almost straight ahead in the distance. We walked along a track with a field on our right, and crossed a stone stile into a field (full of cattle, so put Moll on a lead), and continued through five more fields via stone stiles while Mousehole stretched out down below us, with St Clement's Isle just beyond it.

Mousehole harbour

After the last field, we bore right to a kissing gate in the bottom right hand side of the hedge below a telegraph pole in the middle of a field. This led into a track where we turned left and then almost immediately right down some steps underneath a hawthorn tree. We followed this path downhill with a stream on our left until we came to a junction with two tarmacked paths, where we turned left.

This path led through the old streets and cottages of Mousehole and eventually we arrived back at the Harbour Office and the harbour, where we had a very pleasant time wandering round this old village. By this time I was in need of another drink, so we stopped at the Old Coastguard hotel (dog friendly) which has a very comfortable lounge where we had a cup of coffee before heading back to the van.

The Christmas Lights at Mousehole are now world-famous since they were started in 1963 by a local artist who put up a string of lights along the harbour to cheer things up for Christmas. Everyone loved it so much that two local carpenters made frames for increasingly intricate displays of lights including a serpent rising from the harbour water (which can still be seen today). On December 19th each year the lights are dimmed for an hour in memory of those lost in the terrible Penlee lifeboat tragedy, when in 1981 the lifeboat the Solomon Browne went to help a ship after its engines failed in stormy seas. The lifeboat rescued four people but both vessels were lost in the terrible seas, and in all, 16 people died, including eight volunteer lifeboatmen.

I have done this walk in many different kinds of weather – sunshine, rain and strong winds, but it never fails to delight. There is a sense of the real, very ancient, unspoilt Cornwall here – as portrayed in the Rosamunde Pilcher films – and while I cannot guarantee the weather, I defy anyone not to be delighted by Lamorna and Mousehole. Though if you go out of season, they're even better.

WALK NINE
PENZANCE TO NEWLYN

The area around Penzance has been used in many of the Rosamunde Pilcher films, including *Argentine Tango, Snow Storm in Spring, The Empty House, Summer on the Sea* and *Reflections*, and many of her books feature this area as well, in particular *The Shell Seekers* and *The Day of the Storm*. Rosamunde Pilcher went to school in Penzance, so I like to think of her walking along the Promenade, or walking her dog through Morrab or Penlee Gardens, as we did.

In particular the Egyptian House in Chapel Street, Penlee House Museum and cafe, and Trereife, Trengwainton and St Michael's Mount National Trust Houses were also used for filming, and many of these feature in this walk which starts off along the seafront in Penzance, known as the Promenade.

What you need to know	
Distance	3.5 miles approx
Allow	1 hour 45 minutes excluding food
Suggested Map	OS Explorer 102 Land's End, Penzance & St Ives
Starting point	Jubilee Pool. Grid ref: SW 475 299
Terrain	Mostly streets, some parks
Nearest refreshments	Duke Street Cafe, Newlyn Art Gallery, many others
Public transport	Train and bus stations in Penzance
Of interest	Jubilee Pool, Newlyn Art Gallery, Penlee Museum and Art Gallery, Penlee Park, Morrab Gardens, Morrab Library, Newlyn Harbour and Arthouse
Facilities	At various cafes; public toilets at Wherry Town, Penzance town hall, station and Newlyn harbour

The Walk

To get to Penzance, take the A30 heading west, or approach via Helston on the A394, which was the way we travelled. Arriving in Penzance, follow the signposts to the town centre and there is plenty of parking either along the promenade, or in the car park nearest the Jubilee Pool, along Battery Road, past the harbour.

The Jubilee Pool is open from early June to late October and in addition to swimming, offers yoga, stand up paddleboarding and other activities, and the poolside cafe has proved a very popular meeting place for visitors and residents alike. The pool was designed in the early 1930s by Captain F. Latham, the Borough Engineer, and was opened in May 1935, the year of King George V's Silver Jubilee. The pool is unusual for its triangular shape with gentle curves, and strong white walls that have a dual purpose: they protect swimmers from the strong, offshore winds and also form terraces for spectators.

The pool was extremely popular but by 1992 was so dilapidated that it was in danger of closing. However, the Jubilee Pool Association was formed and it reopened in 1994, following essential restructural works. After the storms of 2014, the pool was once more rebuilt and is stronger and more beautiful than ever, appreciated by all who visit it not just as a local amenity but as a national heritage asset.

The pool will temporarily close in October 2019 to allow for the completion of geothermal installation in November. It will open as soon as possible.

One breezy Sunday morning in November, Viv and I, together with Mollie and Titch the terriers, parked along the promenade and walked past the Jubilee Pool, where the sun shone on the recently painted white and blue of the lido walls, making it look more like summer than autumn. Having admired the pool, we walked along the promenade for a few minutes and then turned right along South Place, a small street leading to a stone archway with 1883 inscribed on it, which in turn leads into the garden below the church of St Mary the Virgin.

We climbed up through the churchyard – "let's have a look around," said Viv. "I wouldn't mind ending up here – you've got an amazing view of St Michael's Mount."

"Except," I pointed out, "that you wouldn't be able to see it if you were dead."

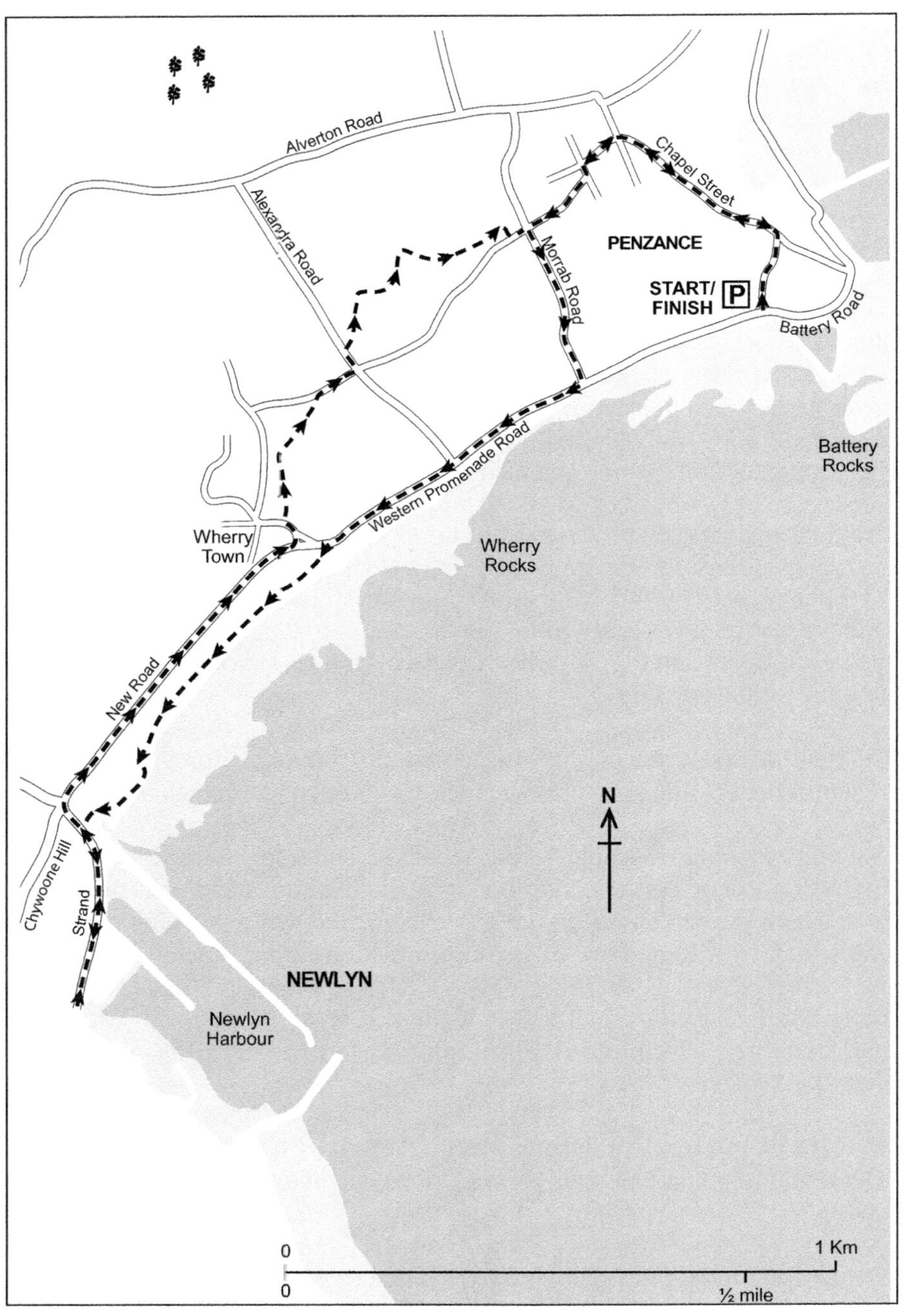

Alverton Road
Alexandra Road
Morrab Road
Chapel Street
PENZANCE
START/ FINISH
P
Battery Road
Battery Rocks
Western Promenade Road
Wherry Rocks
Wherry Town
New Road
Chywoone Hill
Strand
NEWLYN
Newlyn Harbour
N
0
0
1 Km
½ mile

Undeterred, we wandered round this very peaceful place and sat on one of the thoughtfully provided benches, listening to the robins and blackbirds singing. Mount's Bay did look wonderful, with waves whipped up like miniature white horses, all bent on escape. Tearing ourselves away from the view, we continued up through the churchyard, before coming to the church and turned left, into Chapel Street.

Walking along here we came to the Admiral Benbow, a very popular pub that was converted from a stable, the name coming from the book *Treasure Island*. "Did you know that Gregory Peck and the Rolling Stones have drunk here?" said Viv. "And that lead singer from Madness. Can't remember his name."

I didn't know that, but I have seen the wonderful collection of maritime artefacts in the pub that have been rescued from various shipwrecks over the last 400 years. The fine woodwork in the Captain's Cabin restaurant comes from a Portugese ship, while the Lady Hamilton lounge has a ship's figurehead and a cannon, and the upstairs bars have amazing views over Penzance harbour towards St Michael's Mount. The pub is child and dog friendly and has a cosy fire in winter and I could see Viv was tempted.

"No," I said firmly. "It's too early for a drink," so we continued up Chapel Street, past the Egyptian House, a Grade I listed building that dates from around 1835, although there is some dispute about the exact date and architect. It is built in the style of the Egyptian Revival architecture and has been owned by the Landmark Trust since the 1970s.

Almost opposite, we noticed the Union Hotel on our right where I once stayed with my late husband. "It was here that the mayor, Thomas Giddy, announced the great victory at the Battle of Trafalgar and Nelson's death," I told Viv. "Penzance says it was the first town in the country to hear this momentous news and they celebrate every year with a Trafalgar Ball held in the same assembly room, which is now the hotel dining room."

Viv was duly impressed, but also by the quirky shops at the top of Chapel Street – Stekfensters has a wonderful antique/junk collection, while East of Here has beautiful Indian quilts in the window. At the top, the street curves round to the left past Ian Lentern butchers – who sell excellent meat. We followed along Parade Street, past the *Honeypot* cafe, which is well worth a visit for fantastic coffee and home made food. The Acorn Theatre is on the right, a wonderful example of independent theatre, and further along, past

Parade Chambers, we turned left down a small alleyway which leads to some iron gates and Morrab Gardens.

This is a beautiful little sub tropical garden full of plants that have been acquired since the 1880s by many Cornish families including the Bolithos of Trengwainton and the Williams' at Trewidden. Morrab House was built in 1841 by Samuel Pidwell, a rich brewer. By the end of the 19th century, Penzance was an important and popular seaside resort needing a visitors' park, so Penzance Corporation bought the property at auction and built the cast iron bandstand in 1905. The Boer War Memorial statue was erected in 1904 to commemorate the men who lost their lives in the South African campaign.

Morrab Library is also located in the house, one of the few large, independent libraries in the UK, with over 55,000 books on literature, history, biography, antiques, travel and religion. Visitors are encouraged to call in and have a look around, using the Reading Room to browse through the books, in this fine Victorian mansion set in its own private garden.

"I love this place," said Viv. "It always seems warm and sheltered – it's almost magical, isn't it?" Sure enough, the tree ferns and sub tropical plants seem bigger and more extravagant than anywhere else in Cornwall, and if you do

The bandstand in Morrab Gardens

meet anyone, they are always smiling and relaxed. The dogs loved it, too, and scampered in between the huge tree ferns, the bright pink camellias and the reed grasses, enjoying the autumn sunshine.

Leaving the gardens by another south western gate, we turned left into Morrab Road and then down onto the promenade where we turned right towards Newlyn. The promenade was built in stages during the 1800s and finished in 1893, when it was the centre of Penzance nightlife. Norman Garstin's famous painting *The Rain it Raineth every day* depicts the promenade on a blustery wet day in 1889 and now hangs in the Penlee Museum in Penzance: the Prom is still very recognisable now.

On the day we walked it was sunny and blustery with seaweed and pebbles from the beach marking the furthest reach of spray in a storm along the prom. We met plenty of

The Promenade, Penzance

other walkers out for a blow, some with a variety of dogs, some alone, but all smiling into the winter sunshine – you will never want for company on this walk.

Leaving Penzance behind, the village and harbour of Newlyn grew nearer until we reached Wherry Town. There was once a mine here whose entrance was on some rocks below, but which was abandoned when it flooded. Further along is Newlyn Green with a children's playground, a bowling green, and plenty of grassed areas for dogs and children to run around in, while the northerly wind billowed around us, and seagulls wheeled and cried above us.

On the edge of Newlyn Green, we came to a magnificent bronze statue of a fisherman casting his line as the boat arrives in port. This more than life size figure was built to honour dead fishermen, as over twenty local fishermen have died since 1980. The sculptor is Tom Leaper, one of the leading artists and designers in the south west, who lives locally.

We were hoping to go to the Newlyn Art Gallery opposite, and enjoy their dog friendly cafe, but it was shut, being a Sunday, so we continued walking until we reached Newlyn itself and found the Duke Street Cafe. "I need something to eat," I bleated, suffering as I do from low blood sugar. So we went inside for a royal welcome - us and the dogs - and spent a pleasant half hour there, enjoying excellent poached eggs on toast, and vowed to go back another time, it was so good.

Having warmed up, we walked down to Newlyn docks, which is one of the

Statue at Newlyn Green

largest fishing ports in the UK with over 40 acres of harbour. The industry contributes millions of pounds to the Cornish economy every year, and all kinds of fishing boats can be seen here from beam trawlers, crabbers and small open boats used for hand-lining mackerel in Mount's Bay.

In the 16th century, the port was destroyed by the Spanish and rebuilt, but today very little of the original Newlyn remains. If you are lucky enough to stay here, it's worth getting up early to see the fish market where the fish are sold. Some go to local restaurants, but most are sold to London, France, Spain and Portugal.

At the end of South Pier is the Bench Mark from which all heights above sea level in the UK are measured. At low tide, the height of the water is such that the sea bottom is 16ft lower than at high tide.

Newlyn was also home to a group of painters known as the Newlyn School, led by Stanhope Forbes and Walter Langley. Other painters included Norman

Garstin, Henry Scott Tuke and Elizabeth Stanhope Forbes and in 1899 Stanhope Forbes founded the Newlyn School of Art which fostered such painters as A.J. Munnings, Lamorna Birch and Laura Knight. Some of these painters are mentioned in *The Shell Seekers* and *The Day of the Storm,* and I like to think of Rosamunde Pilcher enjoying their paintings, as I often do. Many of them feature the sea, in its various guises, in summer or winter, but all have captured that fabulous light that is rarely seen elsewhere in the UK.

Walking back towards Penzance, at Newlyn Bridge you will come to the Newlyn Filmhouse on the left of Newlyn Combe, a recently developed independent art film house which has proved extremely popular. It was once an old fish merchant's, and has been especially welcomed as Newlyn has not had its own cinema since the 1960s when the old Gaiety theatre, originally opened in 1905, closed.

Crossing Newlyn bridge, we came to Jelbert's Ice Cream which is the nearest you will get to homemade ice cream, and only comes in one flavour - vanilla - which is wonderful for someone like me who can never decide what taste to go for. If you want a variation, you can have clotted cream and or a flake on top. The business was started by Jim Glover's grandfather before the Second World War and the recipe is still a secret - it's such a special product that it has to be eaten fresh and can't be stored in the freezer. Try it and you will be transported back to a time when food tasted better and life seemed a lot simpler. This is also the family of Helen Glover, the Olympic rower, of whom Newlyn and Penzance are justifiably so proud!

We turned first right down towards Newlyn Art Gallery, then left to continue back along the prom, but at Wherry Town, just before the skate park, we crossed the road to Lariggan Road which led to the Rotary Boating Pool which was ruffled by miniature waves, the water lapping over the sides. Walking along with the lake on our right, we noticed the grounds of the Cornish Pirates RugbyTeam on the right and continued, crossing the stream. We then followed a public footpath sign which led to a lane on the right where we met several other dog walkers with a variety of dogs.

At the end of this lane we turned left into Alexandra Road, one of the main roads from the prom leading up towards the bypass and the town. It is a long, quiet, wide road with elegant terraced houses on either side, and outside one is a stall which sells flowers - bunches of very early daffodils today - depending on the time of year, and vegetables. "I'm going for beetroot and daffodils," I said, so thus armed, we crossed the road to Trewithen Road and further on this led us to the gates of Penlee House and Gardens further along on the right.

The sun made a welcome appearance, lighting up the autumn leaves, as we entered the gardens. The elegant oak and beech trees provided a jewelled tapestry of yellow, orange and gold against a pale blue sky as we walked along. Around us dogs barked and raced, there was the faint pocking sound of people playing tennis on the hard courts and we took delight in scuffing the fallen leaves with our feet as we walked. It's another friendly, relaxed garden which is delightful in summer as well – I have often taken a book and read, propped against the welcoming trunk of an oak tree.

At the top of this slope is Penlee Museum and Art Gallery and Open Air Theatre. The gallery is a must for all art lovers, featuring many of the Newlyn School artists, and features a very good cafe where you can sit outside in fine weather. The 300 seat theatre provides a unique outdoor space that has celebrated Cornish, national and international performers since 1948, and it's well worth taking advantage of their varied programme in the summer months.

Today, the Gallery was closed, being Sunday, so we walked out of the east gates and turned right into Morrab Road. Walking down this road very like Alexandra Road – wide with tall houses, many of which are guest houses – we noted one with a pair of black and white boots outside. At the bottom of the road we turned left back onto the prom and walked back towards the Jubilee Pool to where we'd parked.

"I suppose Rosamunde Pilcher would know all these streets and some of the places we visited very well," said Viv thoughtfully. "Perhaps she used to have tea at one of the cafes, and maybe she walked along the prom as we did – and swam in the sea on a summer's day."

Rosamunde Pilcher is so good at describing her precious Cornwall, and bringing it to life for us all to enjoy. Many years on, parts of Cornwall remain satisfyingly the same.

PREDANNACK AND KYNANCE FARM NATURE RESERVE

A walk near the beautiful Bonython Manor and Gardens

Bonython Manor and its estate gardens were the location for the Rosamunde Pilcher ZDF film adaptations *The Prime of Life (Blüte des Lebens), Summer of Awakening (Sommer des Erwachens)* and *Anwälte küsst man nicht (Don't Kiss a Lawyer)*. A treehouse was built for one of the films, and retained as a feature of the garden.

Bonython Manor was built in the 1780s, possibly by William Wood, a pupil of the Greenwich architect Thomas Edwards. However, the Bonython family have owned the land since 1277 and left Bonython Manor in the 17th century. The manor had passed to the St Agnes Donnithorne family before then; some had emigrated to South Australia in the 19th century after Nicholas Donnithorne became bankrupt. The family name Bonython changed phonetically several times over the centuries, and various descendants spelled it in different ways.

Bonython is a traditional, mixed agricultural Cornish estate with the 18th century Manor, farm and woodland stretching almost from one side of the Lizard peninsula (the Helford River) to the other (the beach at Poldhu Cove) with each shore just over a mile away.

Sue and Richard Nathan bought Bonython in 1999, but had no idea that they were about to embark on an all-consuming journey, learning and discovering so much about Cornish history and gardens. Bonython has become a way of life for them now, and as a result, one of Cornwall's great gardens has been created.

Bonython Manor is exposed, facing the prevailing south-west winds, but the beautiful Georgian manor overlooks acres of open farmland which stretch down to the sea. The Manor was described by Pevsner as 'exceptionally elegant' and also as an architectural and design triumph.

Mrs Nathan has planted every single plant here, making her dream garden into a reality for everyone to enjoy. A traditional disused stone 'bothy', that was collapsing outside the walled garden, is now a thatched summer house. It was repaired in 2005, and is now a Tea House that looks as if it has always been there. From the apple orchard you can enjoy a wonderful view to the first in a series of lakes.

Every lake has its own atmosphere and planting. Beyond the first lake, which is peaceful and quiet, is a stream, edged with stone found on the estate. In spring, camassias burst forth creating a wonderful haze of blue, followed by irises in profusion which are reflected in the water. The journey continues to the second lake with surprising hot colours, and then on to Quarry Lake, with South African restios, tender plectranthrus, tree ferns and bamboos, all thriving in this atmospheric, sheltered area. The journey back moves past birches, sculpture and a 'chapel'.

Bonython gardens have been landscaped to include a contemporary water feature behind the Manor house, an eighteenth century walled garden with colour-themed herbaceous borders, a traditional Potager garden and an orchard of Cornish variety apple trees. Spring is a wonderful time to visit Bonython, with its traditional Cornish rhododendrons, azaleas and woodland flowers and bulbs. However, colour develops all through the summer with soft harmonies of the herbaceous beds to explosions of hot colour in the South African areas with drifts of ornamental grasses, cannas, rudbeckias and proteas.

I would suggest allowing plenty of time to visit Bonython manor and gardens, but as there are no rights of way over the Bonython grounds, I have chosen a walk not far away that shows Cornwall's coastal path at its best, and also introduces a stunning nature reserve inland. However, this walk can be very muddy if it has rained a lot, so enjoy this walk in dry weather!

What you need to know	
Distance	4 miles
Allow	2 hours
Suggested Map	OS Explorer 103, The Lizard, Falmouth & Helston

Starting point	Predannack National Trust car park. Grid ref: SW 667 161
Terrain	Can be boggy in winter
Nearest refreshments	Bonython Manor and Gardens – Mon-Fri 10- 4.30 from 16 April to Fri 14 Sept except Bank holidays
Public transport	37 bus from Helston to Mullion, walk from there
Of interest	Bonython Manor and Gardens; Predannack Airfield, several beautiful beaches
Facilities	None – nearest at Mullion and Bonython

The Walk

On 19th May 2018, Viv, Titch, MollieDog and I decided not to watch the wedding of Prince Harry and Meghan Markle on TV, but instead headed down to the Lizard to enjoy a walk in some beautiful spring sunshine.

From Helston we took the A3083 signed to the Lizard, then after about 10km we took the B3296 to Mullion, and followed signs for Mullion Cove. Just before the road goes down into Mullion Cove, we took a left turn signed for Predannack and after about 3km southwards, drove over a cattle grid to reach a National Trust car park by a farm.

Getting organised took a little while as it was uncharacteristically hot which meant finishing off the ice creams we'd bought in Mullion and taking bottles of water and sun cream. Finally kitted out, we walked past the donation box for parking at the lower end of the car park and then past Lower Predannack Wollas Farm on the right and Windy Ridge Farm on the left.

We went through a kissing gate to the right of a farm gate and into a grassy track with campion, blazing buttercups and cow parsley on either side, and – "What's that?" Viv, peering at the small brown bird perched in a blackthorn tree.

"A bird?" I said hopefully. That reduced both of us to giggles while we tried to think what it was. "It's not a wren, and it's not a bullfinch. What about a bunting?" I said.

We eventually realised it was a sparrow - not the most obscure of bird to identify, you might think.

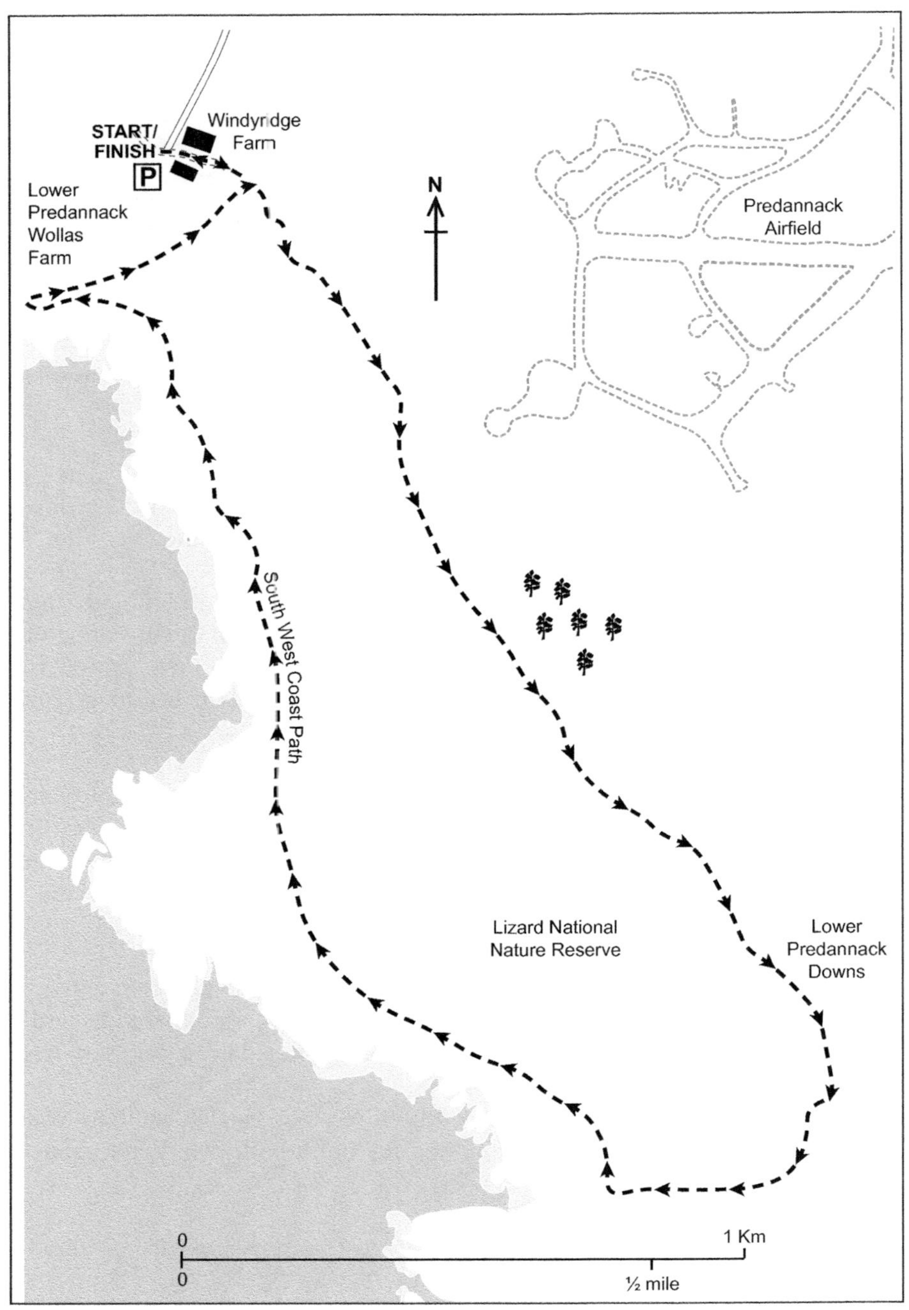

START/FINISH
P
Windyridge Farm
Lower Predannack Wollas Farm
N
Predannack Airfield
South West Coast Path
Lizard National Nature Reserve
Lower Predannack Downs
0
0
1 Km
½ mile

Walking along a marshy section and crossing a stream via a wooden footbridge, we continued along the grassy track which became broad and stony. Ignoring a sign on the right to the coast path, we climbed southwards uphill, veering round to the left, enjoying the sweet singing of skylarks above us, and relishing the clear blue skies.

Looking at the OS map, there is both a footpath and a bridle path running close to each other, and almost parallel going south at this point, but we were on the footpath. The ground was almost like moorland and we could see it had been muddy in winter, but we enjoyed walking on dry turf after a particularly wet winter and spring. Ignoring some waymark signs, a little further on we passed through a wooden five barred gate, then after a few yards we followed a waymark sign over a wooden stile and turned left. This path was cordoned off from a field of cattle by a wire fence, and led to another stile at the end of the path, and a track showing signs of mud that had long dried up.

Coming to a junction of paths, we turned right over a wooden stile next to a farm gate. We walked diagonally left through an area of rough moorland and scrub, heading inland while enjoying the amazing views out to sea to the west and Vellan Head in front of us.

View towards Vellan Head

Having crossed this area of moorland we arrived at a kissing gate and beyond that an English Nature sign saying Welcome to the Lizard Kynance Farm (National Nature Reserve). The Lizard National Nature Reserve, one of 224 in England, is famous for its rare plants, including dwarf rush, wild asparagus and Cornish heath. The increasingly rare marsh fritillary butterfly can be seen here, while chough, peregrine and raven soar above the cliffs, and the heathland puddles support a wealth of rare beetles.

We continued ahead, through the heathland area, heading towards farm buildings in the distance. The turf was dry and bouncy, so the dogs enjoyed it as much as we did, listening to the first cuckoo of the year, and a few skylarks twittering high above us.

At the end of this heathland area we reached a field and about half way through this field, we came to a waymark sign on the left and a gap in the hedge which we walked through, giving us a good view of the aircraft from Predannack airfield ahead of us.

RAF Predannack was opened in May 1941 as a satellite for RAF Portreath and became a fighter base for Spitfires and Hurricanes. 3,600 personnel were employed by 1944, housed in the nearby Mullion Cove and Polurrian hotels. As the war became less intense, fighter squadrons came here for rest and to re-equip, and on 15 September 1945, Predannack opened its gates to the public for the Battle of Britain air display.

A plaque at the entrance, commemorating those who served at RAF Predannack during the Second World War was unveiled on 11 June 2002 and reads: 'Like a breath of wind gone in a fleeting second only the memories now remain'.

Today the runways of this airfield are operated by the Royal Navy, and Predannack is a satellite airfield and relief landing ground for nearby RNAS Culdrose. It is also used by Goonhilly Model Flying Club (with MoD permission) and there has been hobby model flying on the field since the 1950s. The airfield is currently used by the international disaster relief agency, Shelterbox, as part of its Academy for Disaster Relief. At weekends, air cadets learn to fly with the 626 Volunteer Gliding Squadron.

On the west side of the Lizard, away from these operational areas, are Sites of Special Scientific Interest (SSSIs) for their combination of botany (including orchids), zoology (including butterflies and snakes) and geology (bastite and serpentinite).

We turned immediately right to keep the field boundary on our right, until we came to a gravel path which we crossed over to follow a Natural England Permissive Bridleway sign, went through a kissing gate and continued with the field boundary on the right. We noted what looked like an old water tower on our right, and as we continued walking, we saw farm buildings ahead of us also on the right.

Coming up towards the farm we went through another gate, keeping the farm on our right, then came to a Public Footpath sign crossing a track which we followed climbing upwards towards some telegraph poles. We then took a path on the right which headed down the valley, keeping the farm up on our right, and followed a little stream down towards the sea.

Noting the first foxgloves, we continued along a rocky path with the stream tinkling kindly beside us on the left. Mare's tails (cirrus clouds) streaked the pale blue sky above us, while reeds and hawthorn, gorse and brambles clustered on either side of us. It was quiet and peaceful along this little valley, and we felt it had probably not changed in hundreds of years – and hopefully won't.

Picking our way carefully along the floor of the valley which must have once been formed by a glacier, we continued walking towards the sea with high rocks on either side of us, and saw other walkers silhouetted in the distance: it was a perfect day for walking, and proved we weren't the only ones not to be watching the television! Rounding the corner we enjoyed the most spectacular view as the valley opening out to a rich sparkling blue sea that took our breath away.

At the end of this section we noted Gew-graze, or Soapy Cove – named after the soapstone that used to be quarried here. This stone is softer than serpentine, and and was used for early porcelain production.

Soapy Cove is just to the north of where the Spanish Armada ships were first spotted back in July 1588.

Stile with sea pinks

"No chance of me seeing any armadas," said Viv. "I've got the wrong glasses on. Can't see a thing." I had my contact lenses in, so I could see, but she was right – there was no sign of any armada, but a single sailing yacht and further out to sea, a fishing boat with gulls trailing behind it.

Instead of heading down to Gew-graze (it wasn't quite warm enough to swim), we climbed up a steep shale path on our right with equally steep steps which wound inland up the cliff. This brought us to the top of the cliffs where we followed the coastal path, enjoying sea pinks, squill and some huge oxeye daisies, and bacon and egg (trefoil), all blossoming in the warm weather. To our delight we actually saw a skylark on the ground ahead of us – they are very well camouflaged – before it flew high into the sky.

This path goes slightly inland around Pengersick and then Vellan Head and follows the coast round or you can follow another path which leads back across the nature reserve – either affords the most spectacular views up the coast. The coves here have wonderful names such as Ogo Pons and Gersick-an-awn.

Further along, looking over to our right we saw Predannack Airfield on our right while on our left was Vellan Head and in the far distance, the headlands of The Horse, Rill Point, and further on, Lizard Point.

Whichever path you take will eventually lead to a stile which was today covered in sea pinks. Clambering over the stile, and down some well worn stone steps, we noted another sign, on the other side of the Lizard Kynance Farm National Nature reserve and continued walking, meeting several other sun blessed walkers, some perched on the cliff edge drinking a bottle of water and eating snacks, others walking in bare feet or flip flops.

We continued along the coastal footpath with the hedge boundary on our left and a field dotted with campion, buttercups and a few of the last bluebells – very royal colours on this royal wedding day. Around us were the sounds of early summer: the lazy buzz of an aeroplane overhead, the barking of a distant dog and a cuckoo's cheery call.

Coming to another stile we saw a National Trust Predannack sign, then reached a stream where the dogs could enjoy a well earned drink, and I heard a stonechat's distinctive voice calling to us from a hedge on our left. Looking down over the coast, the untroubled waters were blue, aquamarine and indigo, with the white ripple of a leisurely wave sweeping in to George's Cove below us and the sea sparkled like diamonds in the sunlight.

"On a day like today, you wouldn't want to be anywhere else," said Viv, who was due to fly off to Cyprus in a week's time. "Perhaps we'll just stay here."

Walking through a gate gap we continued with the hedge boundary on the right hand side and further

Leading to George's Cove

along noticed a slate plaque almost hidden in the right hand hedge which said, 'Part of this land was bought for the National Trust in memory of the Collins family of Cornwall, their descendant Captain JJR Peirson, DSCRN and his wife Caroline.'

About 25 yards after the Collins plaque is a sign saying Predannack Wollas ¼ mile, Mullion 2 miles, so we followed the path bearing right, inland, away from the coastpath, seeing the Predannack farm buildings on our left, a cluster of bluebells and then more oxeye daisies smiling at us. We took the right hand fork of the path which led to another stile by the side of a farm gate, where we met a lady resting in the sun with her collie sitting beside her.

A grassy path led down to the lane we'd walked in on so we turned left here, along the grassy studded with buttercups, and back up the track to Predannack farm and the car park.

This walk may not be as well known as some of the other walks around Mullion, but you couldn't find a more beautiful example of Cornwall's coastline and wonderful examples of wildlife on the nature reserve where little has changed for hundreds of years. Do take time to go to Bonython for a well earned lunch or tea, and see if you can spot the Rosamunde Pilcher locations you may have seen on film – not forgetting the treehouse and Potager garden.

A walk like this really can lift you up, take you out of yourself, and make you realise why so many people fall in love with the Cornish countryside.

POTAGER GARDENS AND SCOTT'S QUAY

Cornwall's mining heritage

Part of what makes Cornwall so special is its mining heritage, as Rosamunde Pilcher knew well, having been brought up here: from 1700 the main three metallic minerals mined during this time were copper, tin and arsenic.

The metal mining industry helped transform our way of life, providing some of the vital ingredients to form the Industrial Revolution in Britain which, in turn, brought about some of the major technological developments that are in use today.

Steam engine technology was originally developed by Richard Trevithick to pump water out of mines, but his pioneering work enabled the development

Scotts Quay

of steam trains which in turn brought about the mass movement of people and goods. Many other engineering inventions were developed here in Cornwall and exported to many mining regions including the USA, Australia and South Africa: Cornish miners took their skills to at least 175 places around the world.

There are over 200 engine houses in Cornwall which can still be seen today, and the remains of the transport networks developed to serve the mines can be seen on this walk. Wheal Vyvyan was the mine nearest to Constantine, providing employment for many in this area, mining for tin, copper, iron and quarrying for granite. Scott's Quay, also featured in this walk, was used for exporting minerals and stones and importing coal and timber.

What you need to know	
Distance	4 miles approximately
Allow	1 hour 45 minutes walking time – extra for refreshments at Potager
Suggested Map	OS Explorer 103, The Lizard, Falmouth & Helston
Starting point	Potager car park Grid ref: SW 744 290
Terrain	Muddy in parts, a few steep hills
Nearest refreshments	35 bus from Falmouth to Helston getting off at Constantine
Public transport	Bus 442 from Camborne, then walk from the Countryman Inn at Piece
Of interest	Potager Gardens, Scott's Quay, Scott's Wood, Constantine Stores, Tolmen Centre
Facilities	Potager Garden

The Walk

One cold but beautifully sunny day in early December, Ursula, Viv, Titch, MollieDog and I set off for Potager Gardens, near Constantine (not to be confused with Constantine Bay on the north coast). From Falmouth's Union Corner roundabout, follow the signs to Mawnan Smith and turn left, signposted Constantine 5 miles, into Hillhead Road. There is also a small sign

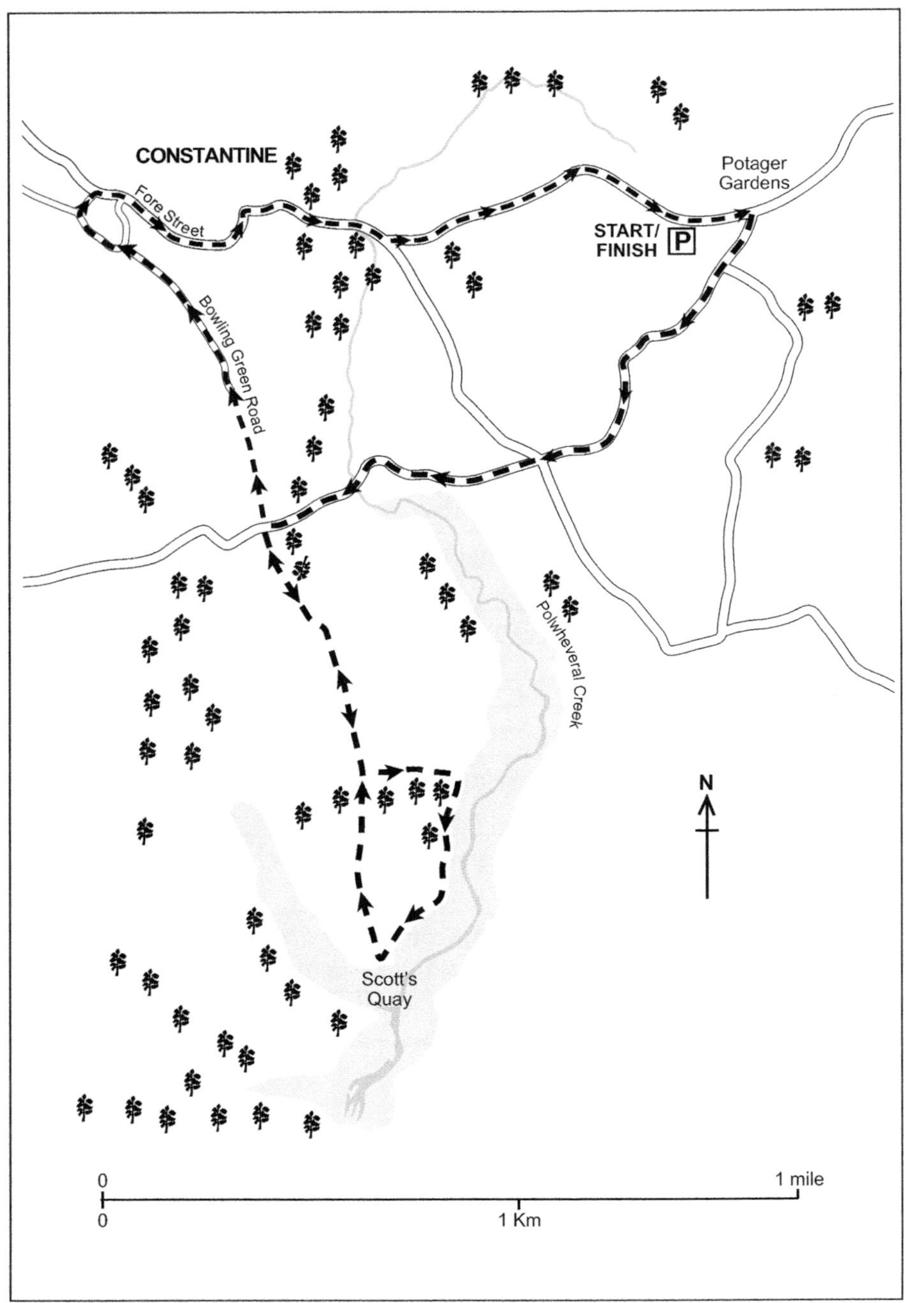

CONSTANTINE
Fore Street
Bowling Green Road
Potager Gardens
START/ FINISH
P
Polwheveral Creek
Scott's Quay
N
0
0
1 mile
1 Km

to Potager Garden here. Continue along the road, through Lamanva, then take the first turning on the left signposted Constantine 3 and another small sign to Potager Garden. Follow this road until you come to High Cross, ignore a small sign on the left to Potager (this is for deliveries), and continue down the road until you come to a large car park on the left, which is the main Potager car park.

Here we noted that the gardens were open 10-5 Tuesday to Sunday and that well behaved dogs are welcomed. We climbed up the path, past some chickens in a fenced off area, and into the gardens which are on different levels. Through an avenue of beech trees, we came to a kitchen garden on the right, with chard, sprouts and other winter vegetables growing, while set back on the left was an intriguing wall made of different lengths of logs.

The next level up provided hammocks strung from trees; ideal for reading in the summer, and various miniature gardens where groups of people gather to talk, write and read in warmer weathers. Today lots of volunteers were pushing wheelbarrows, hosing down tiles and weeding while we walked round the back, past the main conservatory which houses the cafe, into a larger greenhouse round the back. In addition to many plants and trees, this houses a wonderful wooden sculpture of a man standing on one hand, as well as tables and chairs, a ping pong table and seedlings in pots.

Making our way next door to the cafe, we were welcomed by the mellow warmth of the woodburner, and sat down to a cafetiere of fresh coffee and a deliciously moist piece of home made orange and dark chocolate cake.

Here we met Mark Harris, one of the owners of Potager Garden who told us how the present day garden came about.

"Friends of mine, Dan and Peter, lived in Port Navas and drove past this site every day. They saw the sunlight glinting off the roof of the glasshouse and thought they'd ask if they could use some space to propagate plants in. In 2000 they met with the owner and agreed to buy the whole 4.5 acre site of garden centre which had been abandoned for about ten years."

"It was so overgrown it was almost impenetrable. There was a 100 foot glasshouse on the terrace below the cafe which they didn't even know was there. So they started clearing the site which was very overgrown with brambles and mostly nursery stock which had outgrown its pots. They started clearing and planting, hard and soft landscaping, and carving a garden out of this overgrown mess and tangle of plants."

In this greenhouse, which was originally used for propagating plants, they set up a table one end and did teas and coffees. "We rebuilt this building (the conservatory that is now the cafe) three or four years ago so it's now double glazed, and has a woodburner".

The garden has grown very gradually since those early days. "We have made various improvements and continued developing the garden, extended it further down the hill, landscaped new areas, renovated another greenhouse and we've got planning permission to build some new studios. We're a bit of a mix between a garden and a cafe – the site's entirely run as a social enterprise so that any money that's made is reinvested in the site."

"We work with volunteers and are running a little forest school and a dementia group and want to do more work with getting various groups to spend time together in the garden working alongside each other. We're also doing a trial of singing and lunch workshop to see how that goes. We're trying to encourage more community engagement and be here as a community resource and not just as a cafe."

"We've had two companies here both filming documentaries about Potager. They've also asked about using us as a location for a forthcoming Pilcher film and they want to use the vegetable garden so they wanted to know what would be in flower and what would be available next year."

It was so interesting to find out from Mark a little of the history of the garden, but it was winter and

Statue, Potager

daylight would soon be going, so we headed outside, to explore the gardens, which were lit by a gentle ochre afternoon sun, and made our way to the top car park, past some of the studios. Emerging onto the small road, we turned right and continued along the lane. Where the road forks to the left, we continued to the right signposted Trengilly Wartha Inn.

Past Penolva House we noted the most fabulous views out over the fields, dotted with a few winter trees, and down to Polwheveral Creek, the water seeping in silently between the fields, while the whole landscape was lit by the soft glow of winter sunshine set against a clear blue sky.

We passed oak trees with wonderfully twisty branches, like witches' arms in a fairy tale. Heading down a lane with grass growing down the middle, while looking up, we saw a blackbird flying into the lichen covered branches and the tips of hedges sprouting dark brown, fox red bracken and occasional bursts of saffron gorse. The quiet lane dipped downwards more steeply while old oak leaves littered the edges.

The pine trees coming up on our right cast cast golden slanting shadows in the afternoon sunlight, and we reached a junction signposted Polwheveral straight ahead and Trengilly Wartha. We passed some holiday cottages forming part of a beautiful hamlet called Trenant, where we could hear a river flowing at the bottom of the hill. Passing Polwheveral Mill, then cottages with pink roses in the garden, we reached a very old bridge over the fast flowing water, and a lovely old gingerbread type cottage on the left.

The road then climbed steeply up the other side until we came to Goongillings Orchard and Goongillings Farm, then a public footpath sign on the left, by a sign painted on a slab of slate indicating Scott's Quay. Walking along a muddy track, we came to a wooden five barred gate and a cantilevered stile next to it which led to a grassy field with a path leading southwards up the middle and down the other side of the hill.

The view from the top here looks out over a tapestry of green fields, woods and the Goonhilly satellite dishes on the southerly horizon. There are very few buildings to be seen, but as we descended the path we found a notice indicating an ancient settlement in the adjacent field on our right. To reach this, follow the hedge along the top field until you reach a small round enclosure, though there is very little to see now. This probably dates from a few hundred years BC and would have been home to a small community of farmers and their livestock, with small houses, stables and byres. There are excellent views of the creek from where raiders might arrive. Iron was found underneath this site, meaning that this was once an early mine.

The name Goongillings Farm probably means 'downland by the creek' and has been in the family for over 60 years having been bought in 1954. I love the story that the farm once had its own airstrip and hangar, the latter of which is now a hay shed from which the owner, Captain Dick Pugh, flew his own aeroplane during his retirement.

The path turns into a lane, past the hay shed, where we reached another stile and gateway and turned left, down through Scott's Wood which was beautifully quiet, with gold and brown beech and oak leaves underfoot. The dogs had a wonderful time chasing squirrels through the trees, while the sun shone though the branches and we got our first glimpse of the creek in the distance.

We followed a path round to the right which led to a wooden gate into a field, where we walked along the left hand hedge with the creek on our left. This led to another wooden stile (you can lift up the top wooden slat in order to climb over), then another stile through the fields until we reached a junction and turned left through a wooden five barred gate onto Scott's Quay.

The quay was built in the early 1800s by Charles Scott who owned the manor of Trewardreva and much of the farmland and the local mines. He built the quay to move minerals and stones away from Cornwall via a system of merchant schooners. As well as exporting minerals, boats would bring in coal, timber, lime and salt. A hard road was built from behind Constantine to allow horses and carts to carry the materials to and from the quay.

Scott's Wood, with its lovely beech, oak and ash trees, was planted around the same time. In the 1930s Goongillings and the quay was bought by Mrs Hext of Trebah who rebuilt the derelict quay using the remaining stone as a basis and to be used purely as an amenity. She also created a public right of access down the original track to allow access to the creek frontage for local people and the right of way is only to reach the foreshore.

We explored the quay, which is a perfect place to anchor near if approaching by boat, and maybe have a picnic. In warmer weather, it's ideal for sailing, kayaking or swimming. The views from here are amazing: you can see up and down the river where Polwheveral Creek and Polpenwith Creek meet.

As we looked down river at high tide, the sun caught the tops of the trees, colouring them a warm orangey brown. We sat on a bench on the quay and watched a few egrets stalk silently along the foreshore, while above us seagulls wheeled and cried, but apart from that the only sound was the water eddying round the odd rock as the tide came in. Scott's Quay is a beautiful, magical place, and the owner was so right to place a covenant banning any developments. This kind of place deserves to be kept special.

Leaving the quay behind, we headed northwards up the hill back along the inland path with the trees starkly silhouetted against the skyline as the sun sank below the hills and the temperature began to drop. Along the route we noticed a series of angular, somewhat eerie statues made of tall thin branches painted white, which seemed to be pointing the way. At dusk they looked almost menacing, definitely spooky, and we hurried past as the moon rose against the darkening sky.

Through another gateway, we walked down into Scott's Wood and noted beautiful pine trees silhouetted against the twilight. Heading downhill, we arrived back at the muddy track we'd walked in on and retraced our steps back past the hay shed, where we smelt the lovely piney scent of freshly chopped wood. Looking up, I noticed a lone aeroplane left a white trail, as if it were unzipping the sky.

As we reached Goongillings Farm we crossed the road, climbed up a cantilevered stile opposite, marked by a Public Footpath sign, and walked northwards along the middle of the field, heading for another stile directly opposite. This led to another field where we followed the path uphill as Constantine church and village loomed up ahead of us.

Walking through a gap we followed a faded yellow waymark sign towards the church, past a little green bench looking out over the fields into another well used lane, popular with dog walkers, until we reached the outskirts of Constantine village.

The settlement of Constantine grew up around the church. Mineral extraction led to a massive increase in population and during the 19th century the village expanded down what is now called Fore Street. The main industries of the parish were agriculture, mining of tin, copper and iron – the largest mine being Wheal Vyvyan – and quarrying granite.

Skyline, Constantine

The former Methodist chapel, now the Tolmen Centre, was bought by a social enterprise, Constantine Enterprises Company, in 1998 and now offers a wide range of films, theatre, social and other cultural events including an international guitar festival. Constantine Stores, in Fore Street, is famous for its huge off licence, with over 700 different whiskies and hundreds of fine wines. In September 2006, Constantine won the Calor Best Village in Cornwall competition and in 2007 Constantine was also judged the Best Village in the West of England, in the Business Category.

Walking past a red bin on the right, down an alley which led round the back of some houses, we turned left, and then coming to a junction at the end of Fore Street in Constantine village we turned right, down the road, which is narrow so be careful. We continued down the hill, with very high banks on either side and the moon shining through the oak and beech trees.

This steep and narrow road led us back over a bridge and some beautiful old houses, up the hill, past a house with a little stall selling chicken and duck eggs, and continued up the hill back to a sign saying High Cross and just past there was the main car park to Potager Gardens.

Scott's Quay and Potager Gardens are a reminder of the Cornwall that Rosamunde Pilcher wrote about. She may not have visited Scott's Quay, and Potager Gardens wasn't in existence when she wrote her books, but I have a feeling she would love both as being part of the true Cornwall.

FALMOUTH

Pendennis Castle and beaches

Falmouth is one of many picturesque locations for filming Rosamunde Pilcher's stories, including *Seagulls in the Wind* – filmed at Gyllyngvase beach, *A Fork in the Road* – filmed at a private house and *Italian short story.* The university has also featured in many other films, but as they are not shown in Britain, I would be grateful for any German readers comments to enlighten us on Falmouth's part in the films!

Falmouth's beaches are plentiful and beautiful, there are many historical buildings, including a castle, and many other places of historical interest. Falmouth Hotel is an iconic building; one of the first hotels in Falmouth, when it was linked by the new railway in Victorian times. The imposing cream building stands proud at the end of the seafront, making it one of the most recognisable buildings in Falmouth, and Rosamunde Pilcher would have known it well.

View of Gyllyngvase

Falmouth Docks are internationally renowned for their superb boatbuilding work, as are Pendennis Shipyards for their work building and refitting superyachts. The town boasts plenty of shops, a Maritime Museum, part of the university, the Poly theatre and the Phoenix cinema.

De Wynn's coffee shop in Market Street takes its name from a Mr de Wynn who built a hotel here in the 1780s. This covered the site of the two bow-windowed shops, with stables and a coach house at the rear by the wharves. It became a popular meeting place for Packet Ship Captains awaiting orders to take mail to all parts of the globe from the second largest Post Office in England.

William Murdoch of Redruth was the first man in England to light his house with gas in 1784, and Mr De Wynn did likewise. In 1822 he turned the hotel into two shops, both with the unusually large bow windows which are believed to be the largest double bows (with a nine inch bulge) in the country. You can enjoy a wonderful variety of coffees and home made food here: Rosamunde Pilcher may well have visited here for tea, or gone to the theatre at the Poly, nearby.

Near to the Dell car park, where we start this walk, is Arwenack House, the oldest building in Falmouth, originally built in 1385 and then largely rebuilt around 1567-1571 by Sir John Killigrew, the first Governor of Pendennis Castle. At that time it was described as 'the finest and most costly house in the country'.

At this time the Killigrews were the most powerful family in Cornwall and continued living in Arwenack House for about sixteen generations. One of the most notorious family members was Mary Killigrew, Sir John Killigrew's wife, who was one of Cornwall's most infamous pirates! Much of the original building was destroyed during the Civil War when it was the headquarters of the Roundhead Army who were besieging Pendennis Castle, and Arwenack House was rebuilt in 1786. King Charles II persuaded Peter Killigrew to make the town the Royal Mail Packet Station.

Peter Killigrew's son was killed in a duel in the 18th century and his son-in-law Martin took the Killigrew name, but he had no heirs, bringing to an end one of the most powerful dynasties in Cornwall. The house was neglected and fell into disrepair before being restored in the 1980s. It is now a private home and converted into flats.

The Fox Family built several houses in and around Falmouth including Glendurgan at Mawnan Smith, (now owned by the National Trust), the Rose

Hill in Woodlane, (now the main building for the Falmouth department of Falmouth University), and their Falmouth home, Grove Hill House.

The Dell car park, near Falmouth Town station, once contained Grove Hill House's gardens and large fishponds. Further back in time, this was where the Roundheads camped behind Arwenack House during the Pendennis siege, coming with their horses to drink and bathe in a stream.

What you need to know	
Distance	4 miles approximately
Allow	3- 4 hours including visit to castle and coffee
Suggested Map	OS 105 Falmouth & Mevagissey
Starting point	Dell car park Grid ref: SW 811 321
Terrain	Few hills, mostly pavements and beaches
Nearest refreshments	Falmouth Hotel, Pendennis Castle, Gylly Beach Cafe, Swanpool cafe
Public transport	Nearest railway station Falmouth Town or Falmouth Docks; many buses visit Falmouth
Of interest	Pendennis Castle, gun emplacement, hornworks, Falmouth Docks
Facilities	Public toilets at Gylly and Swanpool beaches; also Falmouth Hotel and Pendennis Castle

The Walk

One afternoon in late January, Viv and Titch, myself and MollieDog met for a walk around my home town of Falmouth – or rather, the more interesting parts (to a dog) outside the town. Driving into Falmouth on the A39, go along Dracaena Avenue, over a roundabout and along Melvill Road. Coming to traffic lights turn left along Avenue Road, then first left again into the Dell car park near Falmouth Town station. Parking was £3.50 for 2-3 hours at time of walking.

From the Dell car park we walked out into Avenue Road, turned right up the hill then first left into Lansdowne Road. At the top of this road, and opposite Emslie Road, we reached Melvill Road and turned left, past the Oceanic Hotel

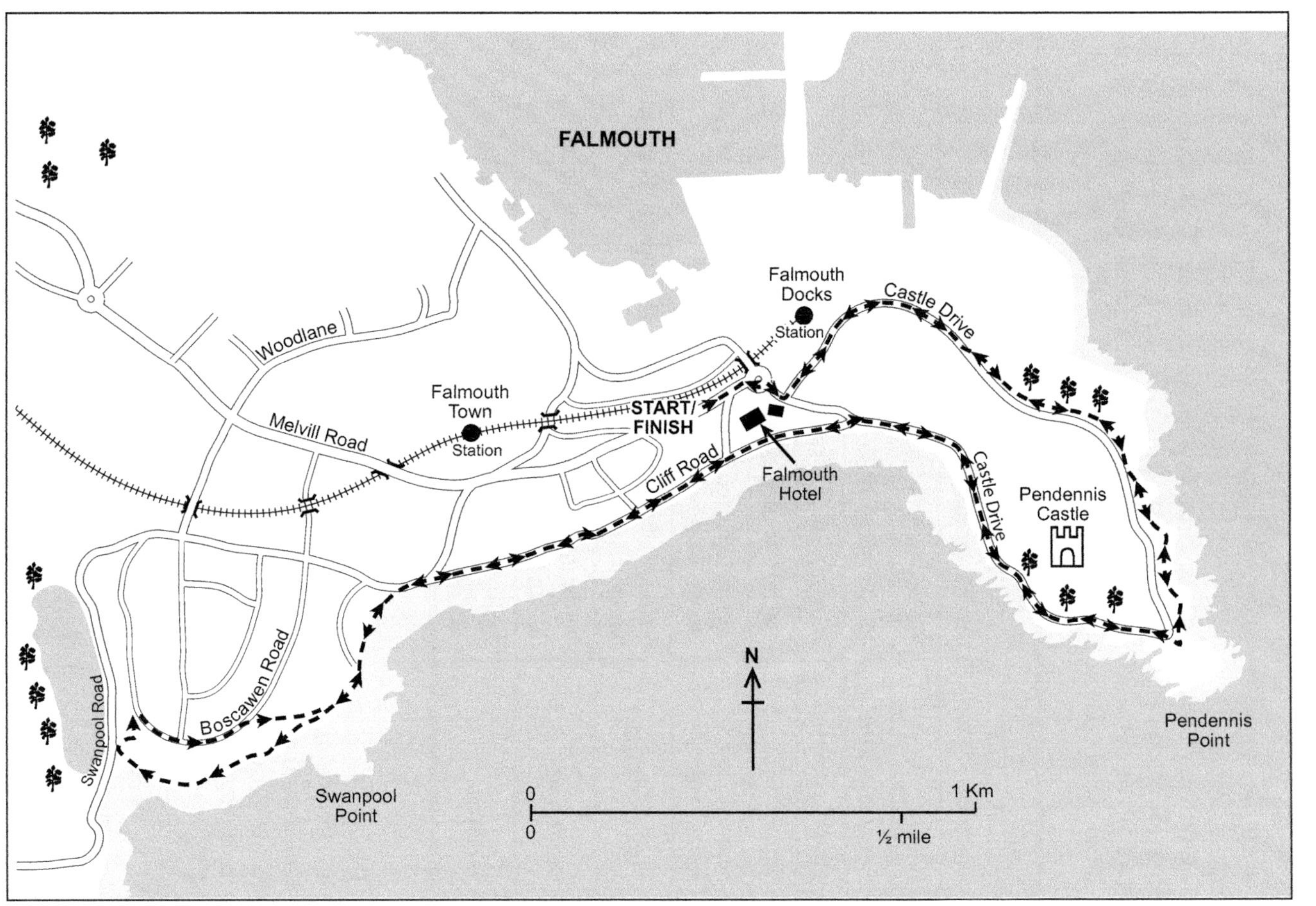

FALMOUTH
Woodlane
Falmouth Town
Station
Melvill Road
Swanpool Road
Boscawen Road
Swanpool Point
START/
FINISH
Cliff Road
Falmouth Hotel
Falmouth Docks
Station
Castle Drive
Castle Drive
Pendennis Castle
Pendennis Point
N
0
0
1 Km
½ mile

until we came to a roundabout below the Falmouth Hotel where we turned right up Castle Drive. Further up we crossed the road to the left hand side where there is a brown road sign indicating Scenic Route to the left and Beaches to the right. We followed the Scenic Route which led along Pendennis Rise, past various houses then a grassy area on the left and further on a large layby to look out over Falmouth Docks.

Falmouth Harbour and the Carrick Roads form the third deepest natural harbour in the world, and the deepest in Western Europe. Lord Falmouth laid the granite foundation stone for Falmouth docks on 28 February 1860, and the first sailing vessel to use the docks in 1861 was the Danish sailing vessel Frederick VII.

When the Cornish Railway arrived in August 1863 this provided a vital transport link to the rest of the country, meaning that the docks could handle more imports and exports. It also meant that many more tourists could visit Falmouth.

Falmouth is the first and last port for those wishing to cross the Atlantic, seeking shelter, repairs or needing to refuel. It stands at the gateway to the Western Approaches and is now an international bunkering (refuelling) port. The docks have played a major role in the ship repair industry for the last 150 years.

The A&P Group Ltd is the largest ship repair and conversion company in the UK, with three shipyards located in Falmouth, Middlesbrough and Hebburn. A&P undertakes a wide variety of maintenance and repair work on commercial and military ships, for both short and long term projects. Today the docks handle all kinds of ships including luxury yachts, warships, tankers and cruise liners.

From the viewing area you can see the huge A&P cranes towering over the various docks, boatbuilding sheds and the ships being serviced – there's usually a cruise ship or two here. The Queen Elizabeth dock holds 128 million litres of water and can be emptied in three hours! Further along are the Pendennis Shipyard boat sheds – the company was first established in 1988.

Opposite, looking north over the water, you will see Trefusis Point, then the huge stretch of water called the Carrick Roads, then St Mawes, before sweeping out into Falmouth Bay. At the end of this viewing area, we crossed

View of Falmouth Bay

over onto the pavement on the right hand side of the road and climbed uphill before turning right by a sign to the Ships & Castles Leisure Centre. There is a large car park here, but we turned immediately left by a sign indicating Public Footpath, and walked along a tarmac path parallel to the road.

This leads to the hornworks, an element of the Italian Bastion system of fortification. These earthworks cross the neck of the peninsular north west of Pendennis Castle: not much is left above ground level as the area was latterly used by the military and then as a car park. Now this large grassy area is used by dog walkers, as well as many magpies, which swooped and dived as we walked, and a few crows, who stalked along the grass like irritated black soldiers.

Another car parking area is found down on our left, and just as the sun came out, ahead of us we could see Pendennis Castle, which has been a major military base for over 400 years and shows the development of coastal defence from Tudor to modern times.

The defences of Pendennis were tested during the first Civil War of 1642-6 between Parliament and King Charles I, over 100 years after Henry VIII built the fortifications here. The King's men fought bravely for five months before food ran short and their commander, Sir Richard Arundell, finally surrendered with honour, marching out with 800 men on 15th August 1646.

A small fort on Pendennis Point discouraged landings by enemy assault troops. The heritage agency Historic England considers Pendennis to be 'one of the finest examples of a post-medieval defensive promontory fort in the country'.

The dogs thoroughly enjoyed their run here off the lead before heading round to the right and the castle entrance which is along a tarmac drive. The castle is only open at weekends in winter, so see website for opening times and prices before visiting. There is so much to see here – and a very good cafe – that it is well worth allowing several hours to explore the keep, the gun emplacements, experience the war time raid underground at Half Moon Battery and explore the Victorian War Shelters where the gunners slept and ate while they worked. The views from the main coastal lookout point are well worth seeing. And the castle is dog friendly, so Titch and MollieDog got their history lesson, too.

Pendennis drawbridge

Having enjoyed the castle, we followed a sign to Moat Walk and headed along the higher path (the lower one, in the moat, was very muddy) which enjoys wonderful views through the trees out to Carrick Roads and the tankers sheltering there. Further along, we had another peep of the castle keep over the walls while Viv tried to impress me with her knowledge of the Civil War. This isn't difficult, as mine is negligible.

We walked down some steps leading downhill on the right from where we could see the famous Black Rock ahead of us in the Carrick Roads. This is a well known navigation mark that roughly divides the entrance of the harbour into two distinct channels; the eastern deep water channel and the western more shallow channel. It is instantly recognisable, and at low tide seals like to sunbathe on the rocks below it.

This path led us to the fenced off gun emplacement area – access is via the castle itself. Pendennis's defences were upgraded in the 1730s and again in the 1790s due to continued concerns about the French invading. In the Napoleonic Wars, the castle held up to 48 guns, and in the 1880s and 1890s an electrically operated minefield was laid across the River Fal, operated from Pendennis and St Mawes and new quick-firing guns were installed.

The castle saw service during both First and Second World Wars, but by 1956 was considered obsolete and was decommissioned. The Ministry of Works cleared away some of the more modern military buildings and opened the site to visitors. Now the castle is managed by English Heritage and in 2011-12 it received 74,230 visitors.

Looking out to sea, a fishing trawler was coming in, with a trail of seagulls behind it, while a few tankers were moored in the bay like sleeping giants. The sea was the colour of slate, interspersed with flashes of indigo blue, royal blue and aquamarine as the sun peeped out every now and then from behind the clouds.

Just after the gun emplacement we turned right and walked down past the Maritime and Coastguard Agency, which is responsible for implementing the Government's maritime safety policy throughout the UK. This includes coordinating search and rescue at sea via the Coastguard, and checking that ships meet international safety rules. The MCA works hard to prevent accidents, to prevent lives being lost on the coast and at sea, to keep ships safe, and to prevent coastal pollution.

Leaving the MCA on our right, we walked down, pausing to admire the amazing views from Pendennis Point car park, over to St Anthony's lighthouse opposite and the Carrick Roads which is the stretch of water where the River Fal and the Truro River meet. "What's that bit over there?" said Viv, pointing to the stretch of water between St Mawes and St Anthony Head.

"That's the mouth of the Perceuil river," I said, pleased to have the right answer for once.

"Percuil as in peculiar?" she asked – to which there is no smart answer.

Looking westwards from Pendennis Point, we could see Swanpool and Maenporth beaches; further down the coast is Rosemullion Head, which hides the mouth of the Helford River. Further west is the Lizard and Porthallow beach and the Manacles Rocks. Manacles, or Maen Eglos in Cornish means 'church rocks' and the church at St Keverne is were many drowned sailors are buried. Its spire can be seen from Pendennis Point on a clear day.

Having explored Pendennis Point (there are always vans selling ice creams should you feel the urge), we turned sharp right and headed north west down the path with the sea on our left and the MCA hidden behind the hill on our right. We continued past a large layby on the left, further down, where divers park as the waters off the rocks below provide good snorkelling. The rocks are also very good for picnics and evening barbecues, as this area catches the sun until late in the evening in summer.

We continued along Castle Drive past a grassy area with picnic tables and a motorcycle monument then came to a junction with some flats on our right and the beaches on our left. We walked along the sea front until we came to the Falmouth Hotel which is a good place for a coffee break – in warmer times the terrace provides a real suntrap, but on colder days the lounge bar is warm and cosy and welcomes four legged friends as well. The Falmouth Hotel opened on 9 May 1865 to cater for tourists who had arrived via the new railway station nearby. The foundation stone was laid on 6 August 1863, by Robert Tweedy and the building cost about £9,000.

The hotel was taken over by the War Department in 1917 to be used as a military hospital. Many famous people have visited here including Prince of Wales (later Edward VII), Beatrix Potter and Simon Le Bon. "Imagine a party with that lot!" said Viv. So we did.

Castle Beach cafe is opposite the Falmouth Hotel but is shut in winter. However, the beach and area outside the cafe is very popular with dog walkers, so our dogs had a joyful scamper along this section of beach before we continued along the seafront towards Gyllyngvase beach.

When the tide is low, it's possible to clamber over the rocks all the way from Castle Beach to Gyllyngvase (or Gylly, as the locals call it). But, "I'm not going over those rocks," said Viv – she broke her ankle badly last year, so it's understandable that she's nervous of repeating that exercise. So we walked along the seafront, watching dogs swimming in the sea, children investigating rock pools and a few brave people swimming.

The seafront is always a sociable place with many people sauntering along, some walking dogs, children on scooters, and those who just like to sit in the shelters and stare out to sea. As we neared Gylly we found a bench painted all colours of the rainbow – very cheering – and almost opposite this we climbed down some steps onto the beach to join the other dog walkers.

Gylly beach and cafe is always popular, whether for walking, eating or drinking. You can also try a range of activities from coasteering to kayaking, Stand Up Paddle boarding (SUPing), badminton and equipment hire. We decided to stick to walking along the beach (dogs are banned from Easter to end of September) and followed the path above the beach which leads round to Boscawen Fields, overlooking Falmouth Bay. There is a fenced off area for those who wish to have dog-free picnics, but apart from that, dogs are welcome everywhere.

As we walked further west towards Swanpool, we looked over to see a large house on the cliffs which was built on the site of the painter Henry Scott Tuke's studio. Tuke was born in York in to a Quaker dynasty in 1858, and came to live in Falmouth in 1860. His happy childhood memories of Cornwall undoubtedly shaped his decision 23 years later to return to live in the county, firstly in Newlyn and then in Falmouth, where he remained for the rest of his life.

Reaching Swanpool beach, we saw several people surfing. In summer there is a row of beach huts, and a very popular cafe that is open all year round famous for its extravagant ice creams. Seating is outside, but blankets are provided for when the weather is cold. On the far side of the road is a nature reserve at Swanpool, which is an important brackish lagoon cut off from the sea. It hosts one protected species, the Trembling Sea Mat which is a rare, primitive animal group made up of tiny sea creatures 1-2mm in size. Many swans and a variety of ducks also live in this Site of Special Scientific Interest (SSSI).

After another run on the beach for the dogs, we retraced our steps up the steep slope then instead of turning right the way we'd come, we turned left up another hill which led to the grassy slopes of Boscawen Fields, several more popular fields for dog walkers. This led back to the path we'd walked in on, and eventually back to Gylly Beach and Queen Mary Gardens which were opened in 1910 and contain a variety of sub-tropical plants such as the colourful agapanthus and giant leafed gunnera. There is a bench here with an inscription by the poet Peter Redgrove, which I love: 'Seasons turn and rivers flow; mourn me hard and let me go'.

At Gylly beach, we walked back along the seafront as far as the Falmouth Hotel. Just past the hotel, the road curves round to the left (Castle Drive) so we followed this round to the left, into Castle Hill, down to the bottom of the hill, and turned left past the bottom of Falmouth Hotel drive into Melvill Road.

From here we retraced our steps along Melvill Road, then crossed the road and walked back down Lansdowne Road which led back to the Dell car park.

Rosamunde Pilcher must have visited Falmouth – and possibly the hotel – as a child if not as an adult, but the town is a perfect location for her films, combining history, beautiful beaches and many fascinating buildings. As well as lots of places to eat and drink there is everything for an urban day out.

TRELISSICK HOUSE AND GARDENS

Trelissick House and gardens have featured in several of the Rosamunde Pilcher TV films in Germany, namely, as Brooks Manor in *Unbridled to Happiness*. It has also masqueraded as the Queenswood estate in *Time of Realisation*, and as the home of Bill Chapman in *Certainty of the Heart*. Trelissick garden also appears in several cycling scenes in *Old Heart not Rust*, with the river Fal in the background. *As From Another Heart* and *Campaign Promises* also feature this very striking house, so it seemed essential to include the house, gardens and woodland walk in this book.

Trelissick Estate is located a few miles outside the cathedral city of Truro, making it a popular place to visit, from coach parties to local dog walkers. The food is excellent, whether for a tasty lunch made from local ingredients, or delicious cakes for afternoon tea. You can also enjoy archery, Nordic walking and snowdrop and daffodil trails in spring.

As we visited just before Christmas, there was a host of festive events such as wreath making workshops, crafts stalls in the stables, visits from Father Christmas, meeting some real reindeer, and Trelissick House was open and decorated with festive cheer: there was even carol singing. The gardens and house were beautifully illuminated from dusk, so there was plenty to enjoy here. There are also unusual places for holiday lets ranging from the water tower to cosy cottages – more information available online.

Several fir Christmas trees cheered the outside areas, dressed in red, gold and yellow baubles, as we wandered around the well stocked shop, then enjoyed some mulled wine in the Crofters Cafe before following the signs to the Woodland Walk, a very popular route with locals, in particular those with dogs.

<table>
<tr><td colspan="2" align="center">What you need to know</td></tr>
<tr><td>Distance</td><td>3.5 miles or longer version 4.7 miles</td></tr>
<tr><td>Allow</td><td>1.5 hours or 2 hours longer version</td></tr>
<tr><td>Suggested Map</td><td>OS 105 Falmouth & Mevagissey</td></tr>
<tr><td>Starting point</td><td>Trelissick car park grid ref SW 835396</td></tr>
<tr><td>Terrain</td><td>Can be muddy in winter</td></tr>
<tr><td>Nearest refreshments</td><td>Crofters Cafe</td></tr>
<tr><td>Public transport</td><td>Bus 493 and 46. Nearest train station is Truro</td></tr>
<tr><td>Of interest</td><td>Trelissick House and Gardens, Gallery, second hand bookshop, Water Tower</td></tr>
<tr><td>Facilities</td><td>Near Crofters Cafe</td></tr>
</table>

The Walk

From Truro, we took the A39 and at Playing Place, by the Shell garage, we turned left onto the B3289 which led through Penelewey, past the Punchbowl and Ladle pub, then we took the next left, signposted King Harry Ferry, and after a couple of minutes, Trelissick Gardens is on the right.

On arrival in the car park (free to National Trust members check for current prices), you can take advantage of the Crofters Cafe, the well stocked gift and plant shop (including my books!), the art gallery which shows work by local and nationally renowned artists, and the second hand book shop has a wide selection of stock.

There is an information board by the car parking attendant's hut, near the start of this walk, so head south over the cattle grid, into the parkland and down the hill towards Channal's Creek.

On the left you will see the beautiful house which was until recently owned by the Copeland family. A villa was first built here in the 1750s and both the house and land was extended in the 19th century by the very rich mining family of Thomas Daniell, and then by Carew Davies-Gilbert, a rich Victorian plant hunter. He added the second floor to the house and spent a lot of time

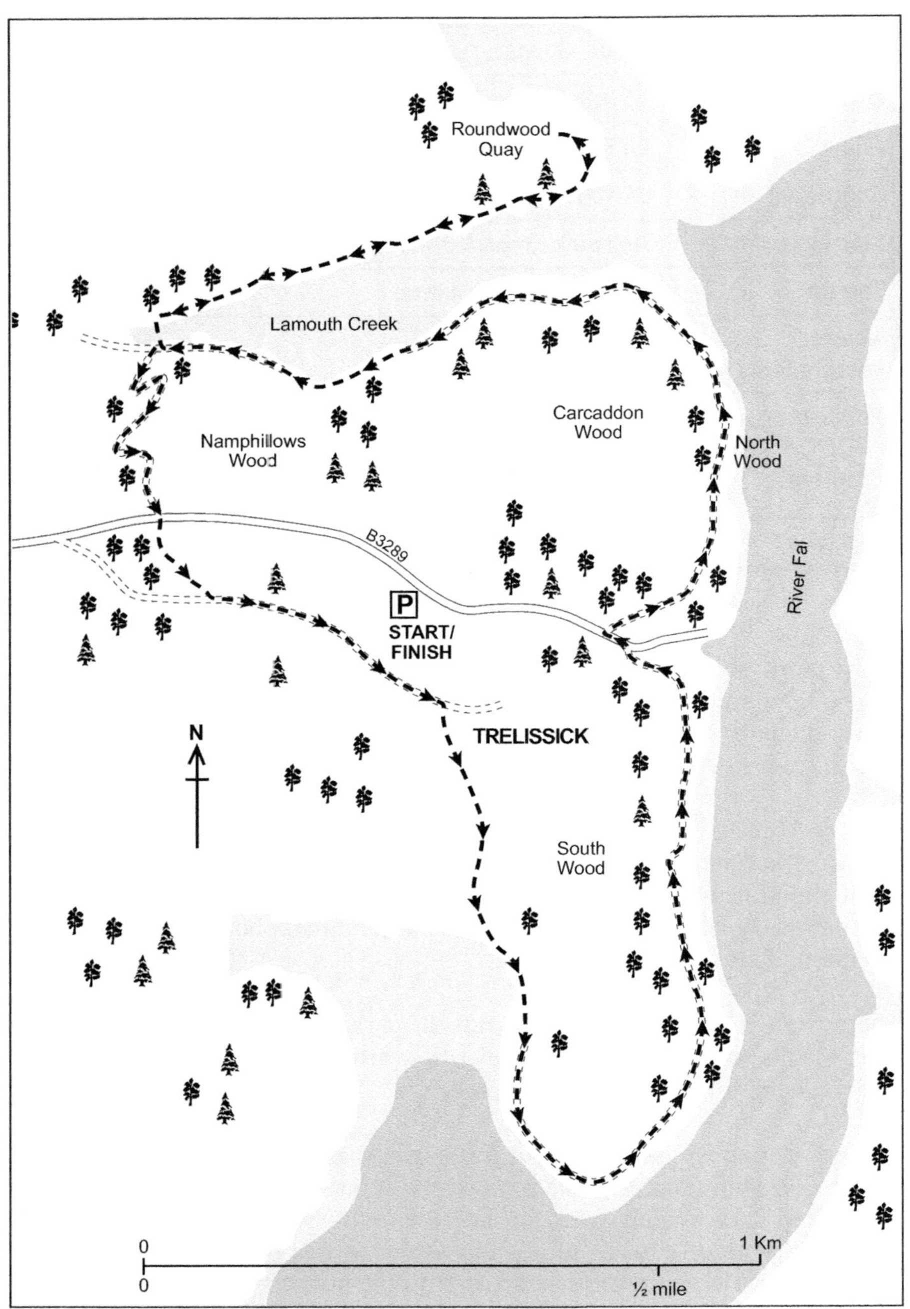

Roundwood
Quay
Lamouth Creek
Carcaddon
Wood
Namphillows
Wood
North
Wood
B3289
River Fal
P
START/
FINISH
TRELISSICK
N
South
Wood
0
0
1 Km
½ mile

developing the garden. When he died his estate was let to Leonard Cunliffe, a former Governor of the Bank of England, who bought the freehold interest in 1928. On his death this passed to his stepdaughter, Mrs Ida Copeland and her husband who was managing director of the china company W.T. Copeland and Sons Ltd.

Many of the flowers painted on their Spode china were grown at Trelissick, and the Copelands developed the gardens north and east of the house. In 1955 Mrs Copeland gave 376 acres of land to the National Trust while the house remained the family home until they decided to leave the main part of the house in 2012, much of which is now open to the public.

MollieDog loves this wide expanse of parkland, and joined other dogs as they scampered through the long grass, while seagulls cried overhead, and a sudden shaft of sunlight changed the water from a dull grey to a lively blue green. In the distance we could just see Pendennis Castle, while nearer to us, a small sailing boat had moored up, and the owner was rowing ashore in a rubber dinghy.

Going through a black metal gate, we arrived down at the bottom of the hill, level with Channal's Creek where the tide was half out, revealing a stony beach where other

Trelissick House

Chanal's Creek

dogs frolicked and jumped into the water. To the left set back from the beach is an upturned wooden boat that functions as a bird hide – inside you can read about different shells and birds on the river at Trelissick – grey heron, little egret and shell duck, teal, mallard and kingfisher.

Continuing past a sculpture of a wooden fish along the shore (in memory of Nina Butler), we walked through another black metal gate along the path, looking over to Mylor Harbour on our right, and Falmouth Docks, even further away. Continuing into South Woods, we saw the first daffodil – amazing on 17th December. The stony path winds round through the trees, with twisted and gnarled branches like an Aubrey Beardsley drawing.

Clearance work has been taking part here, among oak and beech trees to enable the invertebrates and birds – including a rare woodpecker – from around here. Coming up on our right, as the path began to turn round to the left (north), was Turnaware, a suntrap of a beach often used by visiting sailors for barbecues and picnics in the summer.

There are several benches placed strategically along here, should you wish to stop and admire the views, and further along are some pontoons, popular with sailors in summer – I've moored up here in the past which is magic in the summer as it gets the sun till very late in the evening.

Some of the branches along here are festooned with wonderfully rich, long strands of lichen. A few small beech trees still had one or two desiccated, brown leaves, in perfect shape, clinging to their match-thin branches, while the last of the chestnut coloured bracken grew alongside. Many holly trees grow along here, too, for holly has been used in winter since before Christianity: druids wore holly wreaths on their heads – though they must have been somewhat uncomfortable.

Along here are mussel rafts, run by the Duchy Oyster Company. These pacific oysters are grown in bags hanging under the rafts to prevent contamination of the native oyster lays downstream which are dredged by the sailing oystermen in winter.

Ahead we could see the lights of the King Harry Ferry looming ahead on our right. It is one of only five chain ferries in England and the first ferry started here in 1888, connecting the Roseland Peninsula with the Truro area. The alternative route through Truro and Tresillian is 27 miles long, so it's worth using the ferry, which takes over 300,000 cars a year, saving around three quarters of a million litres of fuel.

This part, and the left hand banks of the path along here are covered in beech leaves: you wouldn't think there could be so many different varieties of brown until you see these leaves in all their winter glory. On the right, the banks slope steeply down to meet the river, while the banks on the other side slope up through dense trees to form the boundary of Trelissick gardens.

Along here we came to a signpost on the right indicating the ferry to Truro, St Mawes and Falmouth – we could hear the clanking and chugging of the King Harry Ferry as it reached the Truro shore. Alternatively, you can explore Trelissick House and Gardens via the entrance on the left, or do what we did which is continue along the footpath, down some steps and cross over the road – full of cars waiting to board the ferry – then up more steep steps the other side to continue the walk into North Woods.

More cargo ships were moored up along the river here: massive vessels with huge mooring chains that tether these ships fore and aft. They're a

View down the river

magnificent sight, like enormous ghosts, that often stay here for years. If you listen on a quiet day, you can hear the generators chugging away quietly and occasionally see someone appear on deck.

Regular customers here are the refrigerated ships that bring fruit from the tropics to Europe during the summer but are not needed in winter months. These ships pay hundreds of pounds a week to be moored in these deep water moorings, which brings in useful income for the port of Truro.

As we walked along, we looked down over to Tolverne, or Smuggler's Cottage, which was the assembly point for 27,000 American troops before the D-Day landings, and where General Eisenhower stayed prior to the landing. The cottage was built in 17th or 18th century for fishermen, and contained a collection of items relating to the landings, including Eisenhower's chair. The items were auctioned in 2012, raising a total of £10,000 (Eisenhower's chair sold for £480).

As we approached the entrance to Lamouth Creek, we looked out over a further stretch of the river with a collection of small boats moored up – a small fishing boat, a launch and some sailing boats just waiting for someone to jump on board and sail away. Further on, we came to a sign indicating Roundwood Fort and Quay to the right, and Trelissick to the left.

If you wish, you can make the walk longer by turning off to the right. Walking over a wooden bridge, and through the woods, continue along the path until you reach Roundwood Castle, an Iron Age fort consisting of twin ramparts and ditches, situated between Cowlands Creek and Roundwood Creek.

Climbing down steep steps will lead you to Roundwood Quay, which was built in the 18th Century to export tin mined locally, and copper to South Wales. The quay was used until some point in the 19th century, and ships of up to 300 tons could berth alongside the quay. Retrace your steps until you return to the junction signposted Trelissick where we looked back on the dark green waters of Lamouth Creek – a quiet place that always looks secret and magical.

Following the sign to Trelissick, 20 minutes, we started climbing upwards, noting a beautiful oak tree covered in moss, that had intertwined with a holly tree. I always think it looks like a children's fairytale along here – I can almost see elves and fairies hiding behind the trees, peeping out from the branches, and laughing as they dive into mossy banks, while wizards and other mystical creatures look on.

We heard the tap of a woodpecker on a tree trunk as we walked, and some ducks quacking behind us in the river, while seagulls cried above us. This path climbs steeply, winding uphill with a bench or two at suitable stopping points, before arriving at another metal gate to cross the main road, through a corresponding gate by a lodge, and back into the Trelissick estate.

There are various routes through this little bit of woodland, but we took the left hand path, through a wooden kissing gate and into the parkland and back to the car park from there. This part of the estate is quintessentially English – like parkland from a Jane Austen novel, I think, with ancient oak trees gracing the landscape, sometimes cattle, but nearly always dogs, joyously running through the long grass.

We returned to the car park, where the old water tower was lit up, for Christmas. This tower was built in 1865 as a water reservoir for the house – the height of the tower was designed to provide enough water pressure to put out fires in the main house. Nowadays you can stay here as it has been converted to a holiday cottage with one circular room on each of the four floors, connected by a narrow spiral staircase.

If you visit Trelissick, you will see why it has been chosen for Rosamunde Pilcher's films on television. The grace of the beautiful house, which looks down the steep grassy slope to the creek. The gardens, full of a wide range of plants that range back to Victorian times. The estate with its ancient oak trees, with heavy branches weighted down on the ground. And we are allowed to enjoy all that this wonderful estate has to offer.

ST ANTHONY HEAD

The Battery on St Anthony Head, together with the castles of Pendennis and St Mawes, guarded the entrance to the mouth of the River Fal from Napoleonic times until 1956 and is situated on the Roseland Peninsula, on the eastern side of Falmouth harbour entrance. The National Trust acquired the site in 1959.

St Anthony Lighthouse is one of twelve around Cornwall, now all automated, and was built in 1834 by Olver of Falmouth on behalf of Trinity House, who are responsible for lighthouses in England and Wales. The purpose was to warn shipping about Black Rock in the middle of the channel, and the notorious Manacles Rocks, south of the harbour entrance, off the Lizard peninsula.

The octagonal stone tower of the lighthouse is 19m tall with a two storey keepers' house attached to it; the lantern is 22m above Mean High Water. The light itself originally came from eight oil lamps until it was connected to the power grid in 1954. The present lamp is a 1500W

St Anthony lighthouse

first order fixed Fresnel lens which flashes white and red every 15 seconds; 7.5 seconds on and 7.5 seconds off. The red sector faces south-sou'east as a warning for The Manacles.

Before electrification, a large bell outside the tower was used as a fog warning signal. In 1954 this was replaced by a Nautophone fog horn which has a three second blast every 30 seconds.

Originally, early lighthouses were lit with candles, oil lamps and, later, electricity. But the light was inadequate, and a wider, stronger beam was needed. Around 1821, a young Frenchman named Augustin Fresnel invented a central lens surrounded by prisms, with hugely increased the strength of the light source. As a result, Fresnel lenses were installed in lighthouses worldwide, and are still used today. Essentially, the Fresnel lens is a barrel shaped array of lenses circling the light source. Up to 80% of the light is captured by the lens and transmitted 13-20 nautical miles out over water from the top of the lighthouse tower.

At St. Anthony Head there are two small sandy beaches called Great Molunan and Little Molunan. which can be reached in ten minutes on foot from St. Anthony Head. Access to the Great Molunan is accessible via a short steep slope.

The area around St Anthony Head and lighthouse has been used in several Rosamunde Pilcher films: in *Arrows of Love,* in the introduction of *Old Hearts do not Rust,* and in *Evita's Revenge,* Anna and Peter take a boat ride in front of St Anthony's Head.

What you need to know	
Distance	**3.5 miles**
Allow	**2.5 hours**
Suggested Map	**OS 105 Falmouth & Mevagissey**
Starting point	**National Trust car park, St Anthony lighthouse. Grid ref: SW 848 313**
Terrain	**Coastal path uneven in places**
Nearest refreshments	**Bring your own**

Public transport	Truro station 20 miles away then taxi; Western Greyhound bus 550 to St Mawes
Of interest	St Anthony lighthouse, Battery and surrounding buildings; bird hide; stunning views across Falmouth Bay; Place Manor, St Anthony church; St Just in Roseland
Facilities	St Anthony Head

The Walk

From Truro, Fiona, MollieDog and I set off one sunny Saturday in July to take the A39 to Playing Place and followed signs to the King Harry Ferry. We crossed the river on the ferry, followed the B3289 and turned left, then after a few minutes turned left again onto the A3078. After Gerrans, we continued south, took a narrow lane on the left to St Anthony Head and parked in the car park which is free if you are a National Trust member or £2.50 at time of parking.

Walking to the far end of the car park, we passed the right turning to the lighthouse and continued straight ahead signposted to Portscatho, walking past several cottages on the left which are owned by the National Trust and used as holiday lets. This narrow path leads past the toilet block and passes around the site of the old gun emplacement before following a path through gorse, blackberry flowers and blackthorn bushes, showing the first signs of early sloes.

From this headland, we looked out over Falmouth Bay, enjoying incredible views of Pendennis Castle opposite and its sister castle at St Mawes, Falmouth Docks and Black Rock. Further down we could see the beaches of Gyllyngvase, Swanpool and Maenporth, the indent of the Helford area, and further still, the long finger of the Lizard stretching into the shimmering distance.

There were plenty of yachts sailing along on a flat sea and a good breeze, as well as a few fishing boats and several powerboats, interrupting the quiet of the afternoon with throaty roars from their engines. Looking back, we could see the bird hide (the old battery observation post) which is a wonderful place to sit and quietly observe all the wild life of this area – there is a frieze inside identifying various landmarks. In this part of Cornwall it's possible to see kestrels, storm petrels, great shearwaters, rosy starlings and serins, as well as the usual gulls and cormorants.

There are several benches positioned at various scenic places, making excellent picnic spots. We saw few flowers in the hedges, but the white bindweed trumpets and clusters of cream cow parsley adorned the hedges, as well as bracken and pink splashes of campion. Continuing along the outskirts of a large field, we followed the coastal path looking ahead to Porthmellin Head, then further away, Nare Head and Dodman Point to the east, and the 'White Alps' of the china clay country around St Austell to the north east. The skylarks' persistent sweet song shimmered in the air above us, and several tempting looking beaches emerged as the tide fell, revealing patches of golden sand, while down below us was a rock highly populated by small, bossy black cormorants – their weekend meeting place, perhaps?

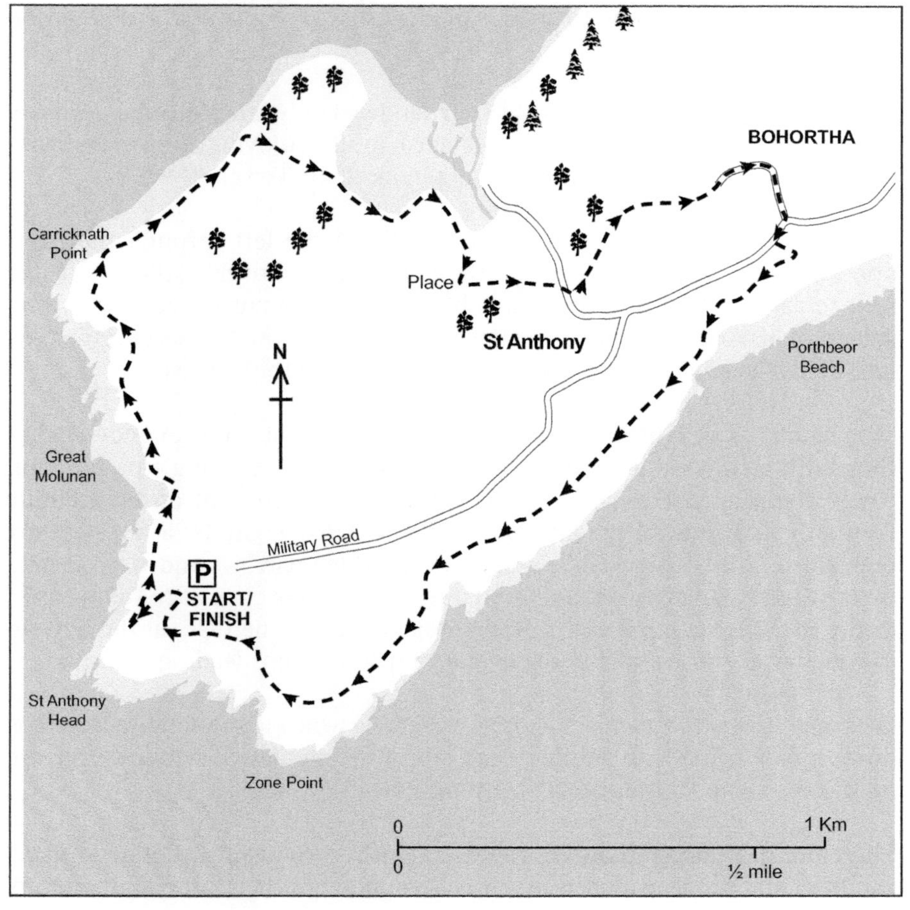

Passing through a kissing gate into another large field, we noted more blackthorn bushes dotted with dusty purple sloes. "It's going to be a good year for sloes," said Fiona. "I must make sloe gin." I kept quiet as I often say this and never do, whereas Fiona is noted for her productivity in the kitchen.

Heading downhill, round Zone Point, we noted Porthbeor beach ahead and Porthmellin Head. The sound of the lapping waves was very soothing as we walked along, over a stile with a lovely example of Cornish stone walling, into another field dotted with small purple thistles. Over another stile we came to a National Trust sign indicating Porthbeor and arrived in a field where we came to a bench next to a path on the right leading down to the beach. Fiona decided to explore but was back sooner than expected. "There's a sign saying the cliffs are unstable and the path's blocked off due to rockfall," she said, so that put paid to our swim.

We sat on the bench instead and ate our sandwiches, while Moll enjoyed a few crusts and a drink of water, and we sat happily enjoying the views: more deserted beaches and a cluster of boats moored off Towan Beach.

Having finished our lunch, we took a path on the left through the field, opposite the path to Porthbeor on the right. This led over a stile in a hedge next to another National Trust Porthbeor sign, into a narrow road where we turned right. A little further along, on a bend, we took the first left northwards into Bohortha where the road did a right angle turn to the west.

This hamlet is delightful and could be straight out of a Rosamunde Pilcher film, with a converted chapel and old school house. Coming to a junction where the road goes round to the right, we went straight on by a Public Footpath sign indicating Place Quay ⅓ mile. Further on, by a red postbox opposite a farmhouse, is an overgrown lane which narrows and after a while we arrived at a junction and followed a sign to the Church of St Anthony down to the left. The path led down the right hand side of the field, at the bottom of which was a stone stile in the hedge with some steps leading to a road.

Crossing the road we came to another slate stile which led to some steep steps down a narrow path to another road, and walking almost straight over, we followed a signpost indicating St Anthony Head 1¾ miles.

The church is larger than I'd expected, with very beautiful stained glass windows and family monuments. It was founded in the 12th century and is always open though it isn't used for worship any more, but according to a notice inside, costs £1.5m every year for essential repairs, so donations are not only necessary but very welcome.

Two sculptures commemorating two members of the Spry family who became admirals in the Royal Navy can be seen here: one of Britannia weeping over Sir Richard Spry, and another of his nephew Sir Thomas. Many other gravestones lean at precarious angles in this church-yard, many of them in memory of young men who drowned at sea in 1889.

The Spry family (presently the Spry Grant-Dalton family) have historic links to Place house nearby, as well as the church, and have lived at Place since 1649. Originally an Augustine monastery in the 11th Century, after the dissolution of 1538 part of the priory was used as a residence while other parts were demolished, with much of the stone used towards building St Mawes' castle and sea wall.

St Anthony church

Being on the Roseland always feels to me somewhere very special and there is the sense that nothing has changed for a long time, which is very precious. The roads are narrow and winding, there is little habitation, and the whole area has a sense of other worldliness. I would think most of it looked exactly the same when Rosamunde Pilcher was a child.

Coming out of the church, we climbed up some steps to the left of the church and headed uphill, walking on a carpet of fallen leaves, before following a yellow waymark sign on the right to follow a public footpath sign indicating the coast path to St Anthony Head 1 mile.

We headed down a stony path surrounded by rhododendron and sycamore trees, and a lovely old wall covered in emerald moss on our right. Reaching a junction at the bottom we turned left and looked down onto the creek, revealed as a muddy basin at the bottom of low tide today. Buzzards gave their distinctive mewing sound high in the air above us, while gulls soared higher still, and curlews cried haunting tunes across the mudbanks.

We followed a sign indicating Coastpath and St Anthony Head 1½ miles (confusingly, after the last one said 1 mile!) and headed along a well trodden path to the right of a large field heading uphill.

At the top was a wooden kissing gate with a waymark sign saying 'St Anthony End of Conservation Area', and on the other side of the kissing gate we were presented with the most wonderful view to the north west over the stretch of water known as the Carrick Roads. It's difficult to describe the sheer awe and beauty of this vast area which today was dotted with many boats of all shapes and sizes leaving ripples along the surface. The St Mawes ferry swam along, cheerful in its blue and white swimsuit, leaving graceful ripples in its wake, while several stand up paddleboarders (SUPs) paddled far out into the channel, enjoying the calm seas. As we followed the path through the middle of the headland, a white whale of a cruise ship hooted loudly, leaving Falmouth port accompanied by the red and blue pilot boat, steering it out of foreign waters.

A group of pine trees loomed ahead of us, dark and powerful figures on the landscape, and the path led downhill to the right of them. As we rounded Carricknath Point, we came to a bench that my friend Tony told me about – this is the perfect spot to admire the view, which we did, while

View from Carricknath

eating snacks. Several walkers stopped for a chat, and we spent a pleasant time drinking in the views, relishing the wide expanse of sea and water. The air was fresh and tangy with a slight breeze, and the air was cool on our arms.

On our right was St Mawes, tucked away like a fairytale village, doused in summer sunshine. Looking over at Falmouth Docks, we could see Penryn climbing up the hill to the right, the turbines at Roscrow turning lazily on the far hill. To our left the cars parked at Pendennis Point shimmered in the sunshine, and beyond we could see the Lizard in the distance, like a foreign land.

The path, now almost due south, winds round the coast, looking down on Great and Little Molunan and several other little coves, many of which are only reachable by boat or on foot. I was once lucky enough to go out for a day's sailing with Tony and we took the dinghy ashore to swim and walk along this part of the coast. It is so beautiful and somehow made more so when you approach it by water.

Great Molunan beach

We came to a detour up to the left – we suspect the cliff path might have fallen down – up some steep steps, at the top of which we turned right along a very overgrown path, meeting a young German family out for a walk. We then walked down more steps, through the pine trees, hugging the coast, and saw Great Molunan, otherwise known as Lighthouse Beach, where I had swum the day before.

Following the coastal footpath around, we came to Little Molunan – a smaller bay, with slightly easier access, but which is only reachable at low tide. We crossed over a footbridge, turned right towards St Anthony Head and walked past the lighthouse's old paraffin store.

Further on, we reached the lighthouse and surrounding cottages which are now holiday lets, so you could have a very different holiday staying in one of these with incredible views. However, be warned – there is a sign near the lighthouse warning that a fog signal with a very loud noise may be sounded in the vicinity at any time without prior warning.

Retracing our steps, we noticed wonderful long tendrils of pale green lichen growing from the walls and trees, then took the right hand fork which led along a steep winding path back to the car park, passing exuberant elderflower trees, sycamores shading the path, and a sprawling buddleia swarming with bees and butterflies.

This part of the Roseland really is incredibly special, and provides the perfect backdrop, not only for Rosamunde Pilcher fans, but for anyone wanting a glimpse of an unspoilt Cornwall. I like to think maybe Rosamunde Pilcher and her family made a day trip here, with a picnic, and maybe also played on these beaches, swam in these coves. She certainly would have loved it, and this is a fitting tribute to the Cornwall portrayed in her books and films.

WALK FIFTEEN
VERYAN

Bronze Age settlers were the first recorded inhabitants of Veryan, leaving one of the largest burial mounds (barrows) in Britain at nearby Carne Beacon, not far from Carne Beach. More recently, the livelihoods at Veryan were farming and fishing, with perhaps some smuggling as well. In the 18th century, the English authorities based a Revenue team at Portloe to try and catch those dealing in stolen goods from the Channel Islands and France.

The Domesday Book of 1086 mentioned Veryan as the manor of Elerchi (now Elerkey) which came from 'elerch', the Cornish for 'swan'. In the 19th century, Jeremiah Trist, Veryan's vicar and land owner, expanded the village's buildings. He persuaded parishioners to to go to church regularly and built two schools – one for boys, which is on the site of the current primary school, and one for girls which is now a thatched house behind the New Inn.

He also built several round houses, inspired by one in St Winnow. Two are at the village entrance by Veryan Green and another two at the Pendower Road entrance to the village. They are all thatched, while a fifth behind the school has a slate roof, and each house has a cross intended to keep the devil from the village. Trist also built Park Behan, a large house overlooking the church as the vicarage was too small and in disrepair.

About a mile outside Veryan is Carne Beacon, supposedly the burial place of the Cornish saint, King Gerennius (Geraint). It is said that his dead body was brought across Gerrans Bay in a golden boat with silver oars, and that the burial mound contains this boat, although there is no archaeological evidence to support this.

Episode 3 of *Karussell des Lebens* was filmed at Broom Parc nearby and at Veryan, while Episode 10 of *Lichterspiele* was also filmed here, as was *Der Himmel Uber Cornwall*.

What you need to know	
Distance	5 miles approximately
Allow	3 hours including refreshment stop
Suggested Map	OS 105 Falmouth & Mevagissey
Starting point	Opposite Veryan church. Grid ref: SW 916 395
Terrain	Few steep hills, a lot of stiles
Nearest refreshments	New Inn at Veryan, Ship Inn or Lugger Inn at Portloe
Public transport	Nearest station Truro; check online for buses
Of interest	St Symphorian church, Veryan, Portloe village and lookout, round houses at Veryan
Facilities	Public toilets at Veryan

The Walk

One quiet, sunny Sunday morning late in November, Mr B, MollieDog and I set forth, over the King Harry Ferry, to Veryan on the Roseland Peninsula. We drove through Philleigh before turning left onto the A3078 then first right and arriving at Veryan. We drove past the pub, heading downhill and parked on the left by a holy well, next door to the primary school and opposite the church. Limited parking is available in the street, when the school is in use.

We decided to explore the church of St Symphorian opposite: Symphorian was a young Frenchman who lived in Burgundy around the 2nd century AD, was tortured and beheaded for refusing to worshop the pagan goddess Cybele, and was buried in a cave. Some 300 years later, a church was built in his honour.

Symphorian has been patron of Veryan church since at least 1281, and looking at mediaeval documents, it's thought that the name Veryan could be a corruption of Symphorian; from Severian through St Verian to Veryan.

Emerging from the Norman church, the sun lit up the tombstones in the churchyard as we walked back onto the road and turned right, where we found a Public Footpath sign indicating to Portloe via Trewartha. This led through

Veryan church

the Water Gardens opposite Veryan Parish Hall. These were very tranquil, reminiscent of Monet's Water Gardens with a beautiful wooden bridge. We didn't cross the bridge but continued walking straight on with the church on our right, into a children's playground, while jackdaws cawed noisily above us.

Crossing the stream via a tiny bridge we headed uphill, treading on a carpet of fallen bronze beech leaves, over the stream again, and up over a stone stile which led into a field, the bottom part of which was extremely muddy and churned up by cattle.

We climbed diagonally left up the field, towards a stile in the far top left by a line of beech trees. From here there is a fabulous view back over Veryan, the fields and a huge manor house encircled by a stone wall. Going through a metal gate, we walked through a small wooded area, then through a metal gate and into another field, heading towards a clump of pine trees.

These trees are at the end of someone's garden, and a stone bench has been placed here with the most amazing views down the valley and right over the Roseland peninsula. What a place to sit and think, taking in the glories of nature. Just past here we walked through another metal gate into a lane with several houses and Trewartha Chapel, which has beautiful windows with green stained glass.

At the end of this lane we turned left then immediately right, down a lane with a No Through Road sign which led to the hamlet of Trewartha. Past Well House, we took a public footpath on the right, past a few cottages, an old water pump and then at the end of this lane, past Jasmine Cottage, we went up over a steep stile in the end hedge and into a field.

Walking past a beautiful old barn, about a third of the way along the end hedge we climbed over an old cantilevered stile by a yellow waymark sign.

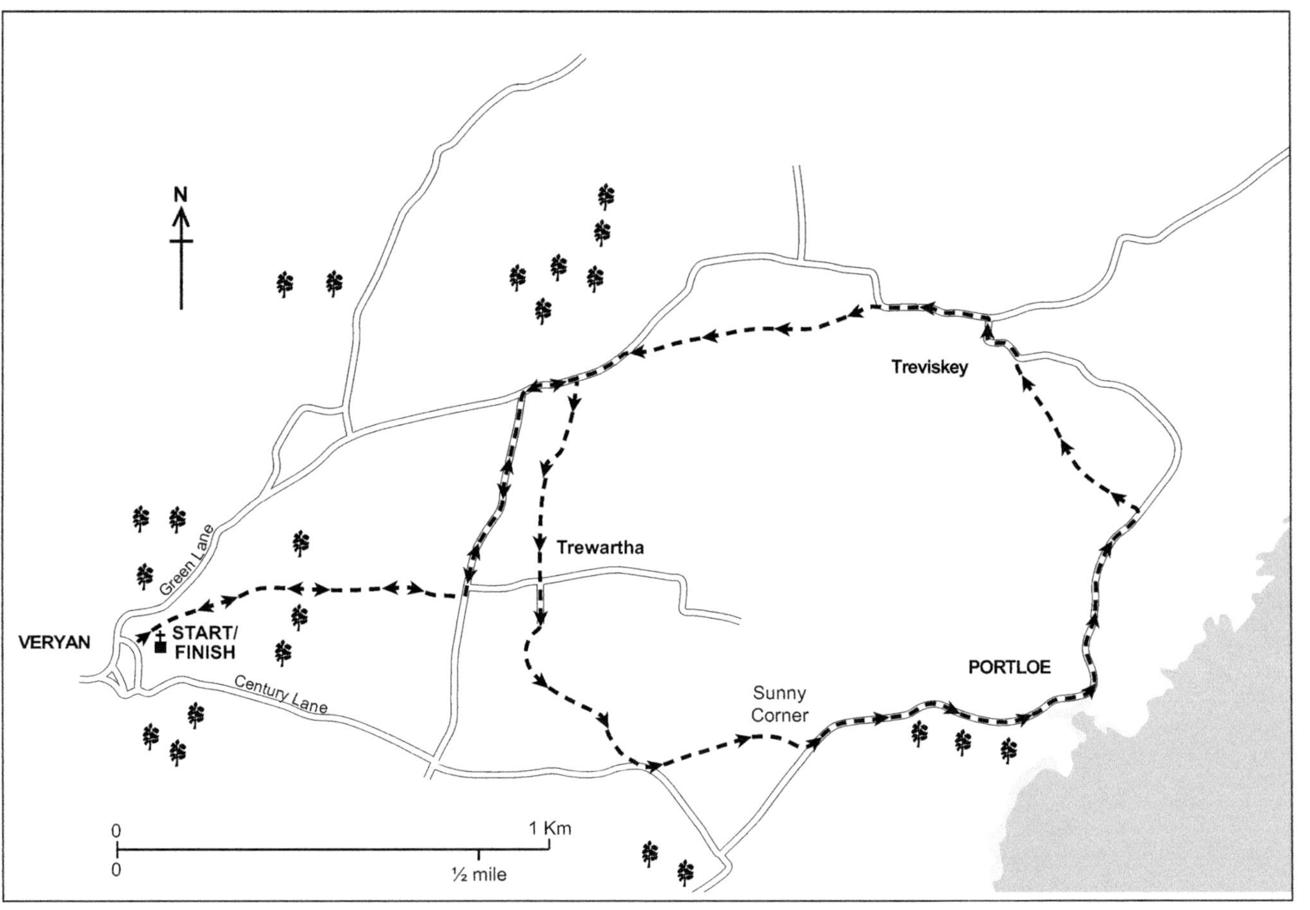

N
VERYAN
START/FINISH
Green Lane
Century Lane
Trewartha
Treviskey
Sunny Corner
PORTLOE
0
1 Km
½ mile

This landed us to a slightly boggy area, then we walked through this next field heading uphill towards a farm.

On the left hand hedge, before the farm, we found a small gate and another yellow arrow waymark sign and a stile which led us into another field where we turned right along by the stone wall towards a five barred gate. We walked past farm buildings, while birds sang in the trees around us.

Here we met a very friendly terrier who turned out to be called Boris, who wished to accompany us. Despite trying to dissuade him, he insisted on following us to the end of the lane where we turned left by a large pine tree and found a pathway leading to another stile into a field with a large rubbing stone in the middle and stunning views down to Portloe and Veryan Bay.

The path was evident across this field, down to a stile on the right hand side of the hedge about two thirds of the way down. At this point Mr B felt he must send Boris back home as, while we were more than happy for him to come with us, he might get into the habit of following strangers.

Having despatched a reluctant Boris, we crossed over the stile and into another field, following the left hand hedge down to an almost hidden path at the bottom, and over another stile. We crossed over the next field which led to another stile in the right hand side of the hedge. This brought us to the road opposite a house called Innis Carne, where we turned left down a steep, narrow road into Portloe.

Coming to the Ship Inn, we went in for a drink – this is a very hospitable pub that is dog friendly, with good food and a wonderful selection of bottled beers. There are also plenty of black and white photographs of Portloe and its inhabitants from several hundreds of years ago, as

Portloe

well as a lot of maritime memorabilia. In the 17th century this building was originally a fisherman's cottage and became a pub at the end of the last century. It's only five minutes from the sea, and has three bedrooms upstairs if you wish to stay here.

After our ginger beers, we strolled down to the cove which is still a working harbour – there were two fishing boats on the slipway on our visit. Next door to the slipway is the Lugger Hotel, which was originally a 17th century smuggling inn and has been named Best Seaside Hotel by the *Sunday Times*.

We continued up the hill until we came to a public footpath sign indicating Coastal Footpath to West Portholland. We decided to take a quick diversion up to Portloe Point to see the view and take some photographs from the top of this very steep hill which was reached by walking in between several houses, over a stream and past a beautifully restored chapel on the left, then up a very steep fight of steps. Finally, panting a little, we reached a viewpoint at the top which had also been the flagstaff, though there was no sign of this any more.

From this vantage point we looked down the coast to Dodman Point in the west and Nare Head and Gerrans Bay in the east, drinking in the amazing coastline. After a while we headed back down the hill, to the junction of the footpath sign and the road, and turned right, past a house with a beautifully painted ship's figurehead on the front wall.

Walking up the quiet road, out of Portloe, the road became increasingly steep and we came to a 30 mile per hour sign at Treviskey Hill, next to an old boat planted with flowers and a brightly painted bus shelter. Opposite we found a public footpath sign, climbed over a stile and walked across a beautifully grassy field, with views of green rolling hills as far as the eye could see.

We climbed over a wooden stile, into another field and followed the left hand hedge leading uphill and into the next field with some houses ahead of us. Over another wooden stile, we found ourselves in a tree lined lane with bamboos on one side which led to a lane and the hamlet of Treviskey with a cluster of very attractive old houses. The only noise here was a hedge full of sparrows, shouting their heads off outside a thatched house with a winter flowering cherry.

From the centre of Treviskey we turned left, past Olive Tree Barn, and came to a junction with a very old signpost and opposite Farm Cottage, we turned left while a pheasant squawked behind us. This led to a larger road where we turned left, signposted to the Nare Hotel, and continued along the road to the second public footpath sign on the left.

Climbing over a stile, we followed the left hand hedge while jackdaws argued noisily above us. Soon we

View from Portloe

came to a metal six barred gate, and we continued walking, keeping to the left hand side of the field, towards some houses. At the end of this field, we came to a wooden stile over a fence which led to what looked like someone's well mown lawn, by the side of Well Cottage, then Well House, and we arrived back at the road we'd walked on earlier.

Turning right at the road, we came to the junction by Jago Cottage where we turned left and then first right, back past Trewartha Chapel. On the right was a collection of massive hairy pigs. which Moll was intrigued by, then we continued along the path until we came to the metal gate. Back in the next field, we walked down the hill towards Veryan, enjoying the sky which was full of purple clouds like towering castles.

Retracing our steps, we welcomed the sight of Veryan and spotted some of the round houses, the beautiful old manor house, and finally arrived at the Water Garden and back at the van.

This walk is in one of my favourite parts of Cornwall – the Roseland is always very special to me, as I feel I've stepped back several hundred years. There is a timeless quality to the land, and once I drive off the King Harry Ferry, I feel as if I've left all my worries behind. Veryan is the perfect place to film Rosamunde Pilcher, for it captures a sense of how Cornwall was many years ago – and still is. Somewhere to treasure.

LOSTWITHIEL AND RESTORMEL CASTLE

A very picturesque area of Cornish mining history

The 18th century is famous for being the peak of Cornwall's mining heritage, but mining in Cornwall goes back a long way before that. In order to export tin, the town of Lostwithiel was founded by the Normans about 800 years ago, when the river was wide and deep so ships could moor up along the quay and load tin to go to many European ports. As a result, Lostwithiel became the second busiest port on the south coast of England.

By the thirteenth century, Lostwithiel was the county capital, the administration centre for county affairs and the main stannary town (where tin was refined, assessed, coined and sold). During the Civil War, the town was badly damaged by Parliamentary soldiers and besieged by Royalists in 1644. In the late seventeenth century much of the town was rebuilt, but the church, bridge and the Duchy Palace are all original buildings from the thirteenth century.

Hidden in the old streets, you will find many shops selling antiques, as well as shops selling arts and crafts, lace and patchwork. The former Corn Exchange houses the museum and a fascinating collection illustrating Lostwithiel life over the centuries, and the local library is in a restored mediaeval house.

St Bartholomew church dates back to the thirteenth century, with a distinctive fourteenth century spire, but the tower has been extended with an octagonal spire grafted on. Do go and admire the great east window which is one of the finest in Cornwall.

The Manor House in the Rosamunde Pilcher films *Never Again Class Reunions* was shot at Ethy Manor, near Lostwithiel, and in *Ex and Love* the Royal Cornwall Hotel is at Boconnoc, near Lostwithiel.

<table>
<tr><th colspan="2">What you need to know</th></tr>
<tr><td>Distance</td><td>4 miles</td></tr>
<tr><td>Allow</td><td>2.5 hours to include castle and nursery visits</td></tr>
<tr><td>Suggested Map</td><td>OS Explorer 107 St Austell & Liskeard</td></tr>
<tr><td>Starting point</td><td>Car park by community centre, Lostwithiel
Grid ref: SX 105 599</td></tr>
<tr><td>Terrain</td><td>Several steep hills</td></tr>
<tr><td>Nearest refreshments</td><td>Community cafe, Lostwithiel, Duchy of Cornwall Nursery & Cafe, Royal Oak pub and many other places in Lostwithiel</td></tr>
<tr><td>Public transport</td><td>Lostwithiel train station on mainline from Paddington to Penzance. Buses 83, 12 and 228</td></tr>
<tr><td>Of interest</td><td>Restormel Castle, church and many ancient houses in Lostwithiel; Community Centre, Lostwithiel; Duchy of Cornwall Nursery and Cafe. Restormel Manor</td></tr>
<tr><td>Facilities</td><td>Duchy of Cornwall Nursery cafe; Community Cafe in Lostwithiel</td></tr>
</table>

The Walk

One sunny Sunday in mid January, MollieDog and I met Viv and her dog Titch in Truro and drove east on the A390 towards St Austell, then continued east to Lostwithiel. At the town, we crossed over the traffic lights, past North Street, and turned right at the sign to the (free) car park, near the Community Centre, both of which were busy as an antiques fair was on. So we drove downhill in the car park past the fire station and parked round the back near the park. The Community Centre has toilets downstairs, so we sampled those before heading off. There is also a very reasonable cafe there, but it isn't open every day so best to check before visiting.

From here, we retraced our steps and headed uphill out of the car park to cross the main road (A390) and took the first right (Duke Street) in between a Chinese takeaway on the left and a big cream coloured building on the right. This used to be the Royal Talbot pub, and there is still a sign indicating this, but it's now been converted into flats.

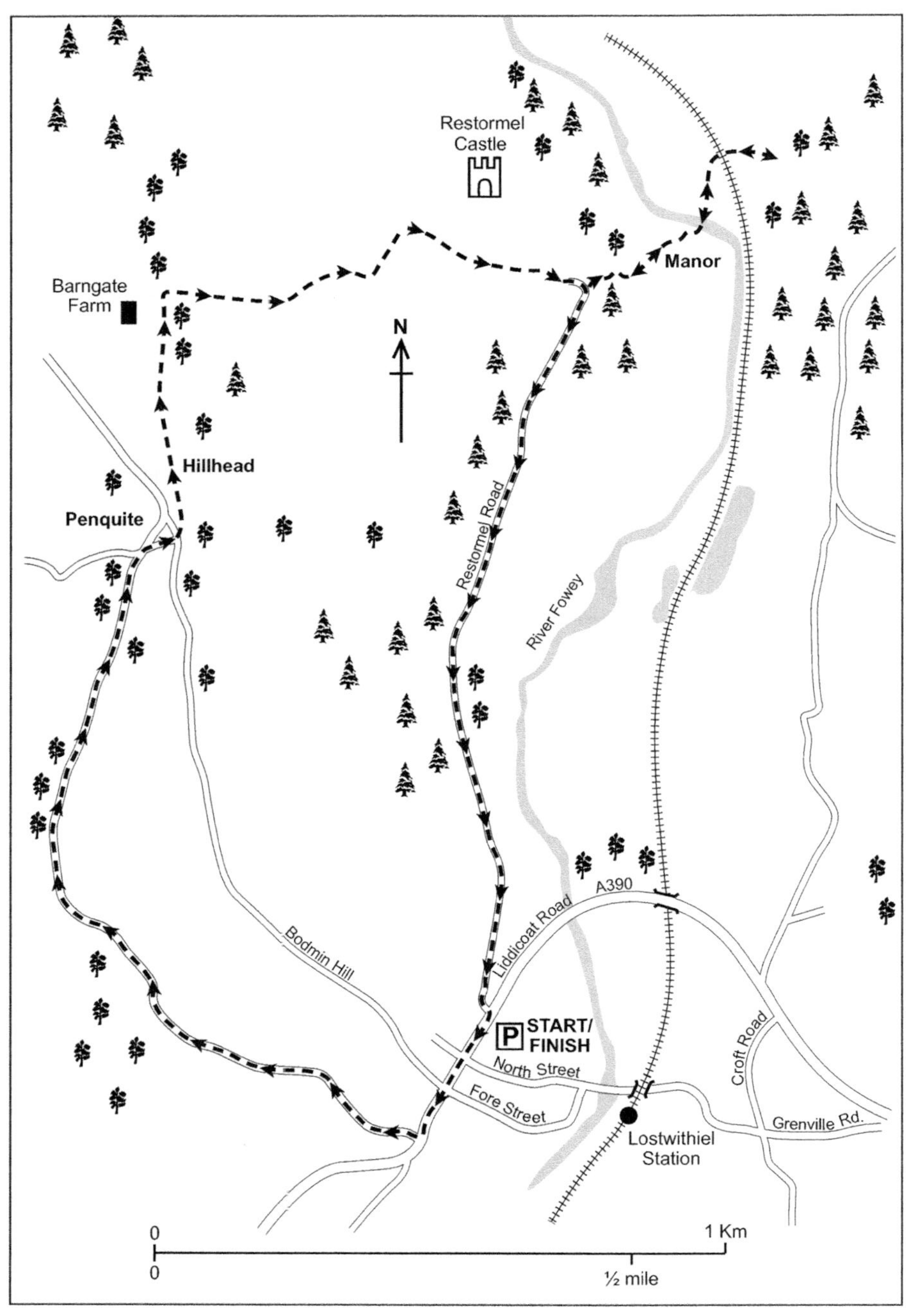

Restormel
Castle
Barngate
Farm
N
Manor
Hillhead
Penquite
Restormel Road
River Fowey
Bodmin Hill
Liddicoat Road
A390
Croft Road
START/
FINISH
P
North Street
Fore Street
Grenville Rd.
Lostwithiel
Station
0
0
1 Km
½ mile

Further up Duke Street we passed the Royal Oak pub which appeared to be popular and could be useful for a drink on the way back, although Lostwithiel contains many eating and drinking places.

"This hill is incredibly steep," puffed Viv as we hauled up Duke Street which was long, narrow and very steep – with no pavement, but it was interesting to see the houses as we walked uphill. At a T-junction we turned right past a house on the right called Mount Pleasant with a beautiful porch of stained glass windows.

"Are we there yet?" said Viv as we continued up the hill, past some new houses, then the school, and just after St Nicholas Park, Private Road, opposite Knights Court we turned left by the Public Bridleway sign in the hedge. Going through a metal gate we walked down a narrow, stony lane where a lot of trees had been chopped down, and logs piled on either side of the hedges. "Those would be good for your woodburner," said Viv. "Shall we take some back with us?"

At this time of year there is little vegetation, but – "Look! First snowdrop!" I said. The dogs had a wonderful time exploring the new smells, and as we walked along on a carpet of wood chips which absorbed the mud, we noted how steep the densely wooded valley is here, with the river thundering down on our left at the bottom of the hill.

Walking through a wooden kissing gate, we passed young spindly holly trees and noticed brilliant yellow gorse flower further down the valley. Then the sun came out, a dog barked, and looking up, we saw the pine trees silhouetted against the sky. The path continued steeply downhill then we passed through another wooden kissing gate and met a narrow road where we turned right up another hill, which grew increasingly steep the further up we walked.

The sun shone onto the fields high up on our right, and because of the heavy rainfall recently, streams bubbled out from the hedges. Walking past Cornish stone walls covered in thick emerald moss we reached the top of the hill, where we turned right and saw a road sign to Lostwithiel. A few yards after this we found a small layby on the left where two cars were parked, and followed a Public Footpath sign through a wooden gate.

The birds were so loud along here they drowned out our chatter. "We'd better learn more about bird song," said Viv. "What do you think they're saying, so loudly?"

"Go away?" I ventured, though they seemed friendly enough, and we continued through another wooden gate, and into a field with a ridge on the left hand boundary. The air here is pure and clear and there is a tremendous, almost giddy-making sense of breadth and depth, of space and height as we looked out over over rolling fields and woodlands. At the bottom of the valley, Restormel Castle peeped out from a cluster of trees, and in the distance a train rattled through the wooded valley.

At the end of this field was a notice indicating a footpath through an open gate and we turned left into a field full of sheep. We walked to the left of the field until we came to another opening which led through a gate into another field of sheep and finally we saw below us Restormel Castle and car park. The countryside round here reminded me more of Devon or Dorset, with its wide expanse of sweeping, rounded hills and wooded valleys.

The thirteenth century circular shell-keep of the castle stands on an earlier Norman mound surrounded by a dry ditch, on top of a high spur beside the River Fowey. It was rebuilt by Edmund, Earl of Cornwall in the late thirteenth century as his luxurious residence and boasted the largest deer park in Cornwall.

Restormel Castle

The bailey has now disappeared, and there is no longer any trace of the large deer park. The Black Prince lived here briefly in 1354 and much later, during the Civil War in 1644, on 21st August, Sir Richard Grenville took the castle from the Roundheads. After this it became ruined and is now in the care of English Heritage – the principal rooms are still in amazingly good condition and the views from the top of the castle wall are magnificent.

If you walk through the base court of the castle, or bailey, approach the shell-keep which stands high on a natural high point in the middle of a circular ditch and bank.

"Apparently, if you look carefully, in the castle grounds and nearby woodland, we might see the Black Pheasant, or Tetraphasis Obscurus," I said – I'd been doing my research. We didn't, but there was plenty of other wildlife – birds, stunning spring flowers and plants all year round. This is also a great place to relax with a picnic and enjoy the amazing panoramic views of the River Fowey and the surrounding countryside.

The wealth of Lostwithiel relied on the Cornish tin trade but ironically it was this that caused the decline of the town when the River Fowey silted up with tin waste: as the port of Lostwithiel declined, so did the importance of Restormel Castle.

Leaving the castle and car park, we walked down a steep narrow road eastwards, at the bottom of which was Restormel Farm and Restormel Estate Office in beautiful old red brick buildings. We turned right, then saw a signpost to 'Duchy of Cornwall Nursery and Cafe 35 minutes', so we continued along the road until we came to another sign on the left to Restormel Manor, and the Duchy of Cornwall Nursery and Cafe.

The public footpath sign led us past beautifully restored old buildings, then into a large field of parkland. Meeting other walkers, one family said, "The cafe is 2.5 miles away," – much further than the half mile indicated on the signpost, but we then met a couple who'd just had lunch there. "It's only a 20 minute walk," they said, so we decided to give it a go anyway. The dogs enjoyed chasing round the graceful parkland by the river, while we walked past the glorious 500 year old Restormel Manor which was built on the site of the ancient Holy Trinity Chapel.

You can actually stay in this Gothic styled mansion, which has three separate wings, and can accommodate up to 18 guests. The manor has been extensively

Restormel Manor

refurbished and great care has been taken to retain the character of the house and its historic features. Prince Charles apparently stays here and walks up to the Nursery, unannounced, twice a year to see how everything is running – no wonder the standards are so high there.

As we are unlikely to stay there, we cast wistful glances at the Manor from behind an iron fence, then continued over a large bridge and walked uphill into pine woods. Being winter, and it having rained a lot, this path was muddy, steep and winding, so wear boots! It's a very popular spot for families, walkers and dogs, particularly those who have recently enjoyed the cafe.

The woods are wonderfully quiet, with beautiful little ferns in amongst the banks, and a variety of exquisite green mosses nestling in the hedgerows. This path continued upwards for about another 15 minutes, following the signs to the cafe and nursery. Further along we turned left, and eventually found ourselves at the top of the hill, in a huge car park for the Duchy of Cornwall Nursery, Cafe and Shop.

Having dogs meant we couldn't have our coffee in the cafe, but there is plenty of seating outside as well as a lovely glasshouse next door which was quieter and full of plants and lights and with very comfy tables and chairs. The food looked fabulous, and a speciality here is the high tea – an array of tiny sandwiches and cakes served on a three tiered dish. We had very good coffee which was served with delicate, delicious shortbread biscuits.

"Let's sit outside," said Viv, as it was warm and we were both hot having walked up the hill, so we sat looking at the fabulous views down the valley. Robins and the odd blackbird came to visit us, eyeing us up to see if there was any food on the go. We also met Ann Wendik-Byfield, a very friendly nursery supervisor (who was German but her English was a lot better than ours), who had worked at the nursery for 21 years and of course knew all about the Rosamunde Pilcher trail.

The Duchy of Cornwall is a private estate established by Edward III in 1337 to provide independence to his son and heir, Prince Edward. A charter ruled that each future Duke of Cornwall would be the eldest surviving son of the Monarch and heir to the throne. The current Duke of Cornwall, HRH The Prince of Wales, is the longest serving Duke in history, and all the proceeds of his estate funds the public, private and charitable activities of the Duke and his children.

The Duchy of Cornwall Nursery was originally a slate quarry, producing forest trees in the late 1960s. It started to sell plants to the public in 1974 and went on to become one of the largest and most well-respected nurseries in the South West, stocking a huge variety of plants, from daffodils and crocuses to apple trees and agapanthus.

Having enjoyed a browse in the shop, which stocks all kinds of things Cornish, we retraced our steps back down the winding path through the woods, over the bridge, past Restormel Manor, through the parkland and finally emerged back on the road.

This is Restormel Road and we turned left, heading south, back towards Lostwithiel with plenty to hear and see along the way – the wind rippled through ridges of pine trees towering in the woods up on our right, sounding like a fast running river, while water meadows full of placid sheep lay on our left. At a hole in the wall we noticed two cock pheasants, vying with each other for some food, and by the river, another train rattled by, taking its passengers deeper into Cornwall.

Lostwithiel bridge

This road was apparently the Royalist route from the castle back to Lostwithiel, but today we walked past Lostwithiel Bowling Club with Lostwithiel golf course as a backdrop. Soon we reached the outskirts of Lostwithiel and arrived back at the main road opposite the car park by the Community Centre. The clock was chiming five as we reached the town, peace was all around us, and dusk was beginning to fall. We could almost smell early spring in the air, and all was right with the world.

PENCARROW HOUSE

Home of the Molesworth-St Aubyn famly

Pencarrow House, situated on the North Cornish coast between Wadebridge and Bodmin, is one of the finest stately homes in Cornwall and was built in 1771 by the architect Robert Allanson. It has been lived in by the Molesworth-St Aubyn family for the last 500 years and and the house is reached by a mile long driveway flanked by beautiful conifers, rhododendrons, camellias, hydrangeas and azaleas.

The house has often been used as a location for Rosamunde Pilcher films including *English Wine* in 2001, when Pencarrow was transformed into a vineyard and all the ground floor rooms were used. In 1998 *The Red Dress* was filmed in the Italian Gardens here, and *The Weekend* and *A Question of Honour* were also filmed here.

The BBC also used Pencarrow to film *Going for a Song* and an American TV company filmed *Hunt for Amazing Treasures*, about a hitherto unknown manuscript by Beethoven that was found among the papers at Pencarrow. This manuscript was sold at Sotheby's in London to raise money for essential roof repairs.

What you need to know	
Distance	4 miles
Allow	2 hours – longer if visiting Pencarrow House
Suggested Map	OS Explorer 109 Bodmin Moor
Starting point	St Mabyn Inn Grid ref: SX 042 732
Terrain	Few steep hills
Nearest refreshments	Pencarrow House; St Mabyn Innn

Public transport	55 bus to St Mabyn
Of interest	St Mabyn Church, Pencarrow House and Gardens
Facilities	Pencarrow; St Mabyn Inn

The Walk

One sunny but cold February, Mr B, MollieDog and I took the A389 towards Wadebridge, then turned right onto the B3266. Taking the second turning on the left, we drove towards St Mabyn and once in the village, into Wadebridge Road. At the crossroads beside the pub, we parked in Station Road.

St Mabyn takes its name from St Mabena, to whom the church is dedicated. She was the daughter of Brychan, the 5th century Celtic King who is depicted in the stained glass of the church as well as on the pub sign. The other saint celebrated in St Mabyn church is St Cecilia who is not a Celtic saint but thought to be of Roman origin. She is supposed to have sung to God while dying, and as a result is now the patroness of church music.

Walking back towards the crossroads, we turned down Wadebridge Road, just before the St Mabyn Inn, then first left before the church. The pub was built in 17th century as a farmhouse which later became a church alehouse and finally an inn. Church Ales were celebrations usually held at Whitsuntide and May Day, when ales were sold to raise money for the Church or good causes within the parish. In the late 17th century, drinking was believed to be sinful, and so the church houses were gradually demolished or used for other purposes.

In front of the church we followed the path along the outside of the churchyard to a gate into a school field. Walking diagonally left, we headed for a gate in the far hedge. This led into another field where we followed the left hedge to another gate in a hedge. Walking through the middle of this field, we followed the line of trees on the left, then a fence and a stile below the houses on our right. These were a mix of old and new, but what intrigued us was what looked like an old manor house - called Woodlands on the OS map - that had in part been restored, but the wing nearest us was completely derelict, with the roof falling in, and windows whose glass had cracked and shattered, with ivy growing around them. This was in complete contrast to the rest of the house, which had carefully been refurbished.

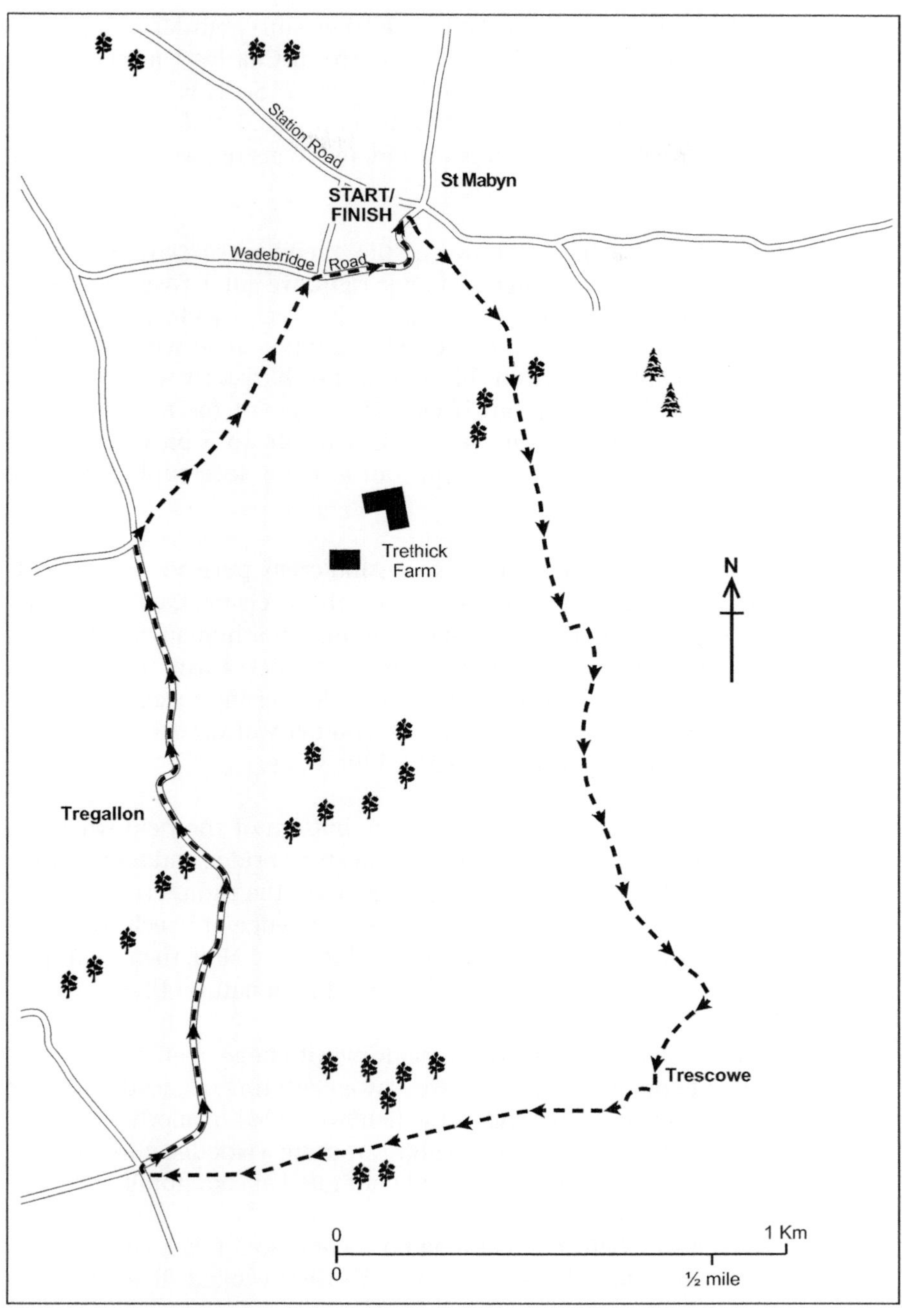

Station Road
St Mabyn
START/
FINISH
Wadebridge Road
Trethick
Farm
N
Tregallon
Trescowe
0
1 Km
0
½ mile

This had all the makings of a Rosamunde Pilcher story, but Mr B had other ideas. "It looks like Miss Havisham's house (from Charles Dickens' *Great Expectations*)," he said. "Shall we go and have a look?" Sadly we were running late, so felt we should pursue this on another occasion. But if any walkers or readers know the reasons behind this dilapidated mansion, we would love to know.

On the left hand side of the fence was a stile, then we crossed a stream to reach a field. Walking with the hedge on our right, we cut across the field to find a stile almost hidden in the far hedge, in between two large trees. The other side of the stile, we found ourselves in another field with clear blue skies above us, and out of the Arctic blast of the north easterly wind, we could feel the warmth of the sun on our backs. The peace of the afternoon was interrupted by an indignant squawk – Moll had put up a pheasant which flapped into the air, evidently much put out at being interrupted from an afternoon snooze.

The countryside around here is full of space and crisp, pure air – large fields with well trimmed hedges, secretive streams with the clearest, coldest water, and very little sign of habitation – neither of animals nor humankind. Looking around, the only building we could see was Trethick Farm. This part of Cornwall is quite unlike the gentler south where I live, or the spectacular rocky cliffs of the north of the county. This is like another world, with rolling hills and the feeling of space echoed by massive blue skies.

We followed the left side of the hedge to the bottom of the field where we turned left, through a muddy area, over a small stone bridge and followed the wall to a waymark by a stone stile in the hedge on the right. From here we walked along the left hand side of the field with a hedge of beech trees, and saw several pheasants clucking as they scurried to avoid Moll, then a whirring of their wings as they took to the air – they don't look natural fliers.

The countryside resembled a Constable painting with huge open fields, bright light and brilliant colours. Further on we saw a clattering of jackdaws as we came to a grassy path at the far end of the field which led to another stile and field where we followed the left hand hedge. Crossing a wooden stile we came to a stream with a wooden boardwalk and continued ahead, uphill.

Crossing another stile before a metal gate we came to a fence and a yellow waymark sign, and crossed over the stile. We then walked diagonally left across the field and over another stile – this walk is not suitable for those with a dodgy hip, "or anyone over 60," said Mr B, as he paused for breath.

We didn't take the stile opposite but walked slightly to the right and found another wooden stile by a metal gate. Through this, we turned right and walked downhill towards Trescowe Farm ahead of us. This settlement dates from early mediaeval times and the first record is from 13th century: the name Trescowe apparently comes from *scawen* which is the Cornish for elder trees.

Going through a gate we turned right onto a track and walked downhill, past the farmhouse where we turned left, and found a pond full of wild irises. The water had overflowed onto the track; as I was wearing wellington boots, I was fine, but Mr B had his army boots on which are in no way waterproof, so he had to clamber over hedges and gates, which caused a certain amount of bad language.

However, having finally reached dry land, we reached a junction where we followed a long, wide track with grass growing down the middle, along the spine of a hill. With Trescowe farm on our right, we looked out over magnificent fields, while the trees of Trescowe Brake and Pencarrow woods loomed on our left, and Pencarrow House and Gardens appeared ahead of us.

On the right we noticed some yurts – large round tents with chimneys for woodburners – in a large walled area, maybe for glamping (superior camping). Next was a tennis court and a beautiful walled garden with espaliered trees, and an area for camping. Walking through a wooden gate we reached Pencarrow House where tickets for the house are available in the car park to the right of the Way Out signs. Guided tours are available during the main season but please check website for opening times and prices as the house and gardens are shut in winter.

Pencarrow has many paintings by the noted artist Samuel Scott and some beautiful examples of period furniture and porcelain. The house has ornate wood panelling, a rococo ceiling and a stunning cantilevered stone staircase.

Trescowe Farm

Pencarrow House

Unfortunately we were too early in the year to visit the house and gardens – they open at the end of March – but we did peek through a gateway into the glorious gardens, and caught a glimpse of the house, which looks equally impressive, so do pay a visit – it will be more than worthwhile.

The politician Sir William Molesworth designed and laid out the 50 acres of gardens which contain more than 600 kinds of rhododendrons and at one time just about every

Pencarrow drive

type of conifer that can be grown in England. The Grade II listed gardens include a sunken Italian garden with a quatrefoil fountain, an icehouse, an ancient Cornish cross and a grotto, which is believed to have been a place for clandestine rendezvous. The Monkey Puzzle tree was named after a visiting friend declared that the tree's unusual branch formations would 'puzzle a monkey'.

From the Way Out signs we followed a beech lined drive with horses grazing peacefully in a field on the right, while the long afternoon shadows slanted onto the grassland. At the end of this drive are some beautiful old oak trees, and we turned right into a small lane following a sign to St Mabyn 2 miles. There are steep hedges on either side of this quiet lane, with primroses and snowdrops peeking forth from the ferns and brambles; out of the sun, the temperature dropped very quickly.

Heading north back towards St Mabyn, on our left was a densely wooded area like a thicket with catkins and ash trees with very straight, slender branches. Further on were more ancient oak trees with twisted branches, as the lane led steeply upwards and we saw a lot of wild garlic on either side of us. This is best used in early spring before it flowers, but unlike domestic garlic, the leaves are used rather than the bulb and the leaves are quite delicate so can be used in large quantities for cooking. If you're not sure what to gather, just remember that if it doesn't smell of onions/garlic, it isn't, so don't pick it!

Coming to a junction to Wadebridge pointing left, we saw a public footpath sign on the right by a gate and followed the right hand hedge to a stile. From here, we could see St Mabyn church in the distance, and crossed the next few fields and stiles heading towards the church tower and trees. Finally we came to a granite stile by a Public Footpath sign which we climbed over and into a lane opposite a beautiful house with a red front door, and we were back in St Mabyn village.

Just past Watergate House opposite, we turned left and walked along a lane round the back of the village. Further along, we saw the entrance to the school playing fields, which we could have walked through if we hadn't had a dog, but as we did, we continued walking ahead, along the road, where we turned right at the end and this brought us back to Station Road, where we had parked.

This was a really magical walk in a part of Cornwall I don't know well, that is stunningly beautiful. Pencarrow House is a real tribute to the county, as is the land around it, and no wonder that the Pilcher films have been shot here – and I'm sure will continue to be in the future. It's a treat to visit the less populated parts of Cornwall, and see how the country was in Rosamunde Pilcher's day.

LANHYDROCK HOUSE AND GARDENS

Lanhydrock House, near Bodmin, is one of the biggest and most impressive of Cornish country houses, with large servants' quarters, beautifully landscaped gardens and 1,000 acres of wooded parkland.

This is the perfect country house and estate, with the kitchens, nurseries and servants' quarters giving a good example of what life was like 'below stairs', while the spacious dining room and bedrooms are truly elegant. Visitors can pick up a house trail to explore the 50 rooms open to the public: the 17th century plasterwork ceiling in the gallery is well worth seeing, and a rare book collection and a Steinway piano can be found in the 17th century Long Gallery. There are many cycle routes and walks throughout the woods and the rest of the estate.

The Lanhydrock estate originally belonged to the Augustinian priory of St Petroc at Bodmin but during Tudor times, with the Dissolution of the Monasteries, the estate was bought by Sir Richard Robartes, a wealthy tin trader from Truro, who apparently gained his peerage by giving the Duke of Buckingham (a favourite of James I), a sum of £10,000. He started building the house in 1630 but died a few years later, and his son completed the house in 1651; the estate remained in the Robartes family until the 20th century.

In the First World War the family lost many members, including the heir, so the estate passed to the younger brother, Francis, 7th Viscount Clifden. In the Second World War, the house accommodated evacuees and after the war, in 1953, the house and about 400 acres of parkland were given to the National Trust. Only one descendant of the original family survives, living in a cottage on the estate.

The stunning gardens at Lanhydrock provided plenty of scope for filming *Cliffs of Love,* while the house and gatehouse doubled as Penlee House, home of the Hastings family *In Doubt for Love.*

<table>
<tr><td colspan="2" align="center">What you need to know</td></tr>
<tr><td>Distance</td><td>4 miles approximately</td></tr>
<tr><td>Allow</td><td>2 hours 15 minutes including picnic stop</td></tr>
<tr><td>Suggested Map</td><td>OS Explorer 107 St Austell & Liskeard</td></tr>
<tr><td>Starting point</td><td>Lanhydrock car park</td></tr>
<tr><td>Terrain</td><td>One steep hill, otherwise easy going</td></tr>
<tr><td>Nearest refreshments</td><td>Cafes at Lanhydrock</td></tr>
<tr><td>Public transport</td><td>Bodmin Parkway railway station nearby</td></tr>
<tr><td>Of interest</td><td>Lanhydrock house, garden and woodlands</td></tr>
<tr><td>Facilities</td><td>Near car park</td></tr>
</table>

The Walk

One gloriously sunny morning in late June, Steve, MollieDog and I headed off towards Lanhydrock. From Truro we took the A39 northwards and then the A30 heading north east. After the Bodmin turn off (about 45 minutes) we left the A30 at the Turfdown junction via the B3268. At the roundabout we took the third exit and followed the signs to Lanhydrock and car parking – there is plenty, and costs £3 per day at time of walking, or free if you are a National Trust member.

From the car park we followed signs to the house and gardens which led us out of the car park, across a road and through some gates to the Information Centre. From here we walked down the drive, with stunning parkland on either side, and lined with ancient oak, beech and sycamore trees, some of which date back to 1634.

On the day we walked, the countryside looked quintessentially English: people were picnicking in the shade of the trees, while in the distance we could see acres and acres of farmland, fields and woods. It was all very gracious and we could have been walking several hundred years ago: all we needed were some horse drawn carriages and a few deer in the distance.

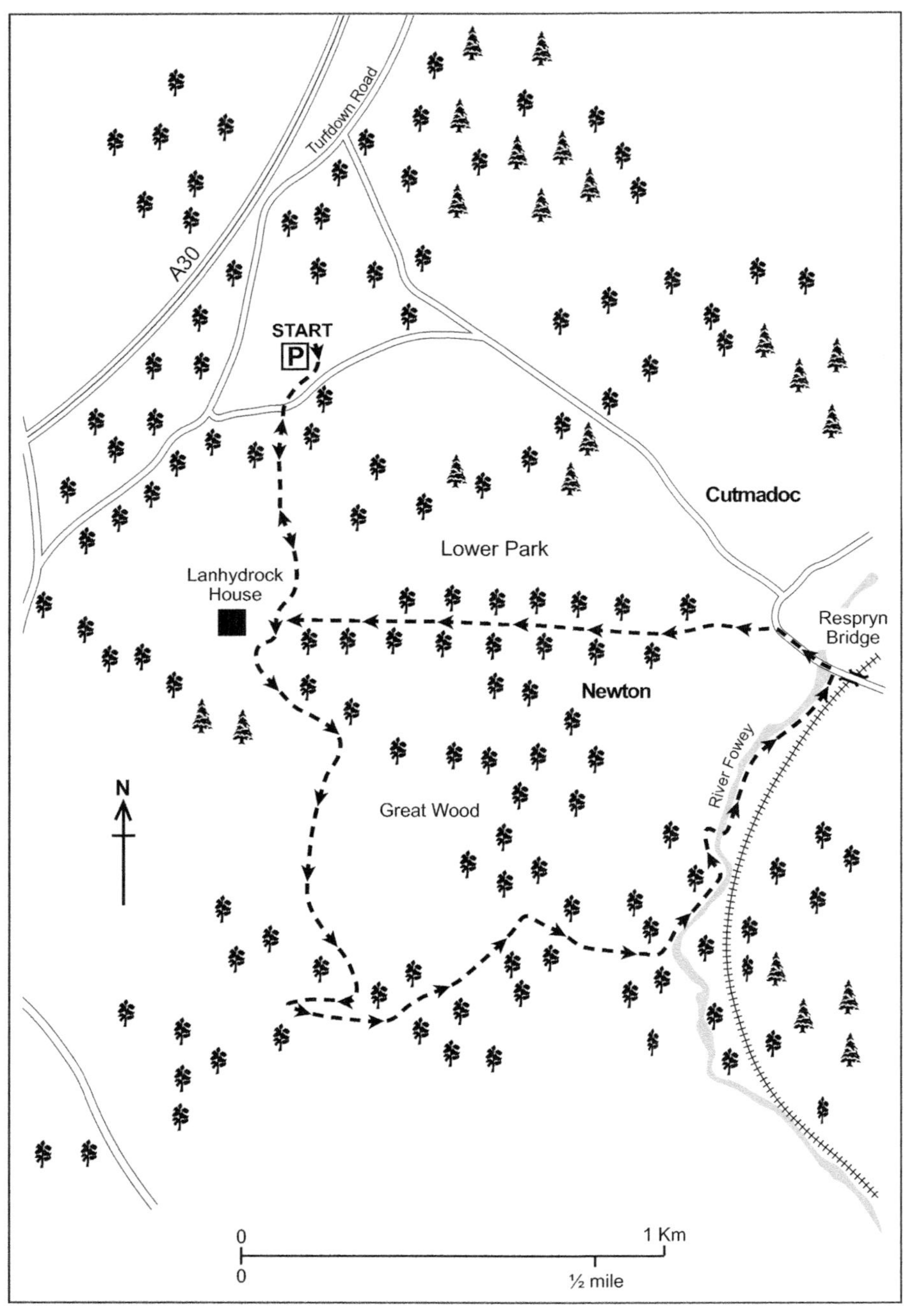

Turfdown Road
A30
START
P
Cutmadoc
Lower Park
Lanhydrock House
Newton
Respryn Bridge
N
Great Wood
River Fowey
0
0
1 Km
½ mile

In fact you may see deer here, but they are shy animals and tend not to appear when there are people or dogs around. Roe, fallow and red deer can all be found in Cornwall and their population has increased tenfold over the last decade. Roe and red deer have pointy, branching antlers, the red deer is larger and has a large white V on its backside, while the roe deer has a small white

Lanhydrock Gatehouse

patch. Fallow deer have flat antlers and an upside down black horseshoe surrounding a white patch on its rear.

Walking down the drive, dodging the unusually hot sun, we eventually arrived at the gatehouse leading to the house and garden. As we approached, the gardens came into view, reminding me of a scene from *Alice in Wonderland*: wonderful examples of yew tree topiary, like massive green boulders. I expected them to start silently moving around, like pieces in a chess game, and to hear the Red Queen shouting, "Off with their heads!".

Today all was quiet, despite the gentle hum of visitors admiring these gardens which were designed by George Truefitt for the owners, Lord Robartes and his wife Julia, to complement the house and for the family to enjoy. These very formal gardens must need a lot of work and include rows of Irish yews and box-edged rose beds, a parterre hedged with box and a herbaceous garden enclosed in a circular yew hedge.

Leaving the house and garden on our right, we found a dark red gate on our left which leads into the Great Wood. This specialises in magnolias, camellias and rhododendrons; many rhododendrons have been cleared, leaving space for amazing bluebell displays in spring. The woods are also home to kingfishers, dormice and twelve types of bat.

Ignoring the path on the left, we went straight ahead, along the main path, lined with many beech trees that provided dappled shade from the intensity of the sun (not something that we normally have to worry about in Cornwall!). Beech trees can last up to 400 years and beechwood ageing is used in the production of Budweiser beer. Young beech leaves can be used as a salad vegetable, tasting a bit like soft cabbage.

The path through the woods was beautifully quiet and shady, away from the bustle of the house. High above our heads, in distant branches, blackbirds and robins sang, joined by the odd pigeon. Passing a sign to the Higher Garden (dogs not permitted) we continued along the main path which curved round to the right, and came to a kitchen garden wall, then the Gardener's Cottage on the left, with rambling roses growing along the walls and stacks of logs piled up outside, ready for winter.

The kitchen garden wall was interrupted by beautiful black wrought iron gates from which we had a tantalising glimpse of poly tunnels, greenhouses and flowers and vegetables growing in abundance.

Further along, we found a wooden fingerpost sign indicating Respryn River Walks, so we followed the sign, admiring the densely wooded valley to our left – pine trees and a tapestry of fields in the distance, and several fields of maize next to us. Birds sang quietly above us, while the river rustled below us on our left.

At a junction, turning left by another Respryn River Walks sign, we walked downhill along another dappled path, passing an old quarry festooned with draping ivy and fronds of ferns of all kinds. The noise of the water grew louder here, and when we came to a gateway where one of the granite gateposts had fallen over, a little further along Steve found a lovely shaded area under the trees, beside the stream. Here we had our lunch and Moll was able to have a paddle and a drink.

Restored, we returned to the lane, admiring the dog roses and foxgloves adorning the hedges, and walked to the end of it, turning right where we saw a sign saying Respryn via footbridge. Further along we found a bench made out of a huge tree trunk, with a plaque saying "Raymond, Rest Awhile" before coming to the footbridge crossing the stream, which had widened to join the River Fowey. To the right of the stream is a sign on a gate to Restormel Castle, but we continued through the woods, with the water chatting away beside us. Fly fishing is popular along here, and there are various platforms for fishermen, as well as benches to rest on.

We were startled by the sudden rush of a train close by: it turned out to be the main railway line from Paddington to Penzance, but when the noise subsided we could only hear a pigeon cooing in the distance, and the river whispering beside us.

Crossing another foot bridge, and walking round to the left, we saw a collection of beautiful dragonflies, their iridescent green/blue wings glimmering in the sunshine. There are sections of this riverbank where dogs are allowed to bathe, but otherwise you are asked to be careful of the bank which is prone to erosion.

We passed another bench made from a huge tree trunk, and fields on our right with woods on the far side that must lead up to Restormel Castle. We walked past more fishing platforms, and beech, sycamore and oak trees with wonderful reflections of the water rippling on the leaves. The afternoon was quiet, punctuated by birdsong and the occasional dog splashing in the river.

Passing a lady pushing a buggy made us realise that this flat section of the walk is suitable for the less mobile and for those with wheelchairs – we also glimpsed a car park through the trees. A fisherman's path runs parallel to this bigger path, and eventually leads to Respryn Bridge, a five arched mediæval bridge spanning the River Fowey. The central pointed arch dates to the fifteenth century and probably represents part of the original construction which replaced the earlier thirteenth century bridge.

Apparently there was a chapel here serving a ford so anyone crossing could pray they would make it to the other side, or give thanks for a safe crossing.

Respryn bridge

The bridge was built in 1300 to carry a trackway between Bodmin and Looe. Respryn Bridge played an important part in the Civil War, as Lanhydrock lay in Parliamentarian hands while Boconnoc was Royalist: King Charles rode over the bridge in 1644, on his way from Boconnoc to Lanhydrock, the two major estates in Cornwall.

In the nineteenth century, with the arrival of the railways, a private halt was built for the Lanhydrock estate, probably south-east of the bridge along a small access road. Although no trace of this is found today, the carriage drive built to take passengers to the new station at Bodmin Parkway can still be followed where it runs through the woods north of the railway line before cutting south across the river to the station.

Walking over the bridge, we soon came to a grassy car park under the trees on the right. "I wonder if there's an ice cream van," said Steve hopefully, for it was very hot. Sadly there was none, though it did look a lovely place to have a picnic, and several families had laid out feasts under the shade of some oak trees. This car park would be ideal for the less mobile, or for those wanting to have a quick picnic by the river without walking too far.

We continued walking along the road and soon found a turning on the left opposite a lodge and a sign to Lanhydrock. A steam train (from the Bodmin and Wenford railway) hooted in the distance, while pigeons cooed and we heard the fat, startled squawk of a pheasant ahead. We passed through a gate by another lodge to the Lanhydrock estate and started walking up the avenue. The trees were an amazing assortment of pale green, lime green, emerald green, dark green; tall trees and their shorter counterparts; ones with afro leaves and some with thinning hair.

After the Civil War, Lord Robartes planted this regal sweep of sycamore and beech trees, leading back to the house, to celebrate his party's victory. Approaching the house from this direction is incredibly impressive.

Half way up this drive we noted healthy looking cattle, so put Mollie on the lead. Most of the cows were with their calves, one of which was stranded on its own in the middle of the drive, calling anxiously to its mum. A large creature came towards it – and us – and we waited, always wary of cows and their calves – then as it grew nearer we realised it was a bull! I held my breath as it ambled past, nudging the calf with its nose, and I scurried up the hill, breathing a sigh of relief.

Lanhydrock house and garden

At the top of this long, steep drive I expected to see deer peeping shyly from distant trees, and a few women in long white dresses with parasols; perhaps men in breeches, but it was rather hot for that. Back at the gatehouse, we turned right at the house to walk uphill through the parkland back to the car park past copper beech, soaring chestnut and elegant beech trees, leaves waving limply in the breeze. Passing the information centre we returned to the car park and cafe where Steve treated us to ice creams, and later made tea in a picnic spot in the car park.

Lanhydrock is the perfect Cornish estate for all lovers of Rosamunde Pilcher – a huge house to explore, carefully designed gardens to enjoy, parkland to picnic in and woods to walk in. There are also numerous cycle routes through the woods at the top of the estate. Together with several cafes serving delicious food, what more could anyone want? I wonder whether Rosamunde Pilcher came here as a child with her family, for a picnic, perhaps, or to explore the magnificent house and gardens? I like to imagine her running around, under one of the oak trees, chasing her dog, perhaps.

I shall remember the magical grandeur of this walk for a long time – for the strong sunshine slanting through the trees, the babble of the river beside us, and summer laughter to cheer a Monday in June.

Also from Sigma Leisure:

Walks in the Footsteps of Daphne du Maurier
Sue Kittow

It is well known that Daphne du Maurier fell in love with Fowey at the age of 18, and soon made Cornwall her home. Her life long love affair with the county is evident: no one can describe the creeks, the moors, the birds or the sea quite like her. Her deft observations of people are wry, accurate and can be frighteningly vivid. *Walks in the Footsteps of Daphne du Maurier* is an unusual tribute to this great and unusual writer. Each of the 14 walks is inspired by her books, characters or places special to her. Some are famous – *Frenchman's Creek*, as the setting for the novel of the same name – while others are less familiar, such as Stowe Barton near Bude – the starting point for *The King's General*. Walks vary from 3 to 7 miles, have concise directions, clear maps, and essential information: length, refreshments and places of interest. This third book in Sue's series is unique for her personal style, the in-depth research, delightful details, the flora and fauna, and excellent photographs. This is a special book to keep and pore over – for walkers and armchair adventurers alike.

£8.99

Walks in the Footsteps of Winston Graham's Poldark
Sue Kittow

Walks in the Footsteps of Winston Graham's Poldark features 12 walks each associated with a different Poldark location from the books, a character, or where an event was filmed for the TV series. Winston Graham was so good at evoking the real landscape of Cornwall, the Cornish people and the unpredictability of the Cornish weather. Feature in page turning plots and empathetic characters, and you have a winner, which the Poldark books have proved to be.

Enjoy these walks and learning more about the Poldark places, characters, and history. Each walk includes details of maps, refreshments, history, points of interest and clear directions and sketch map. What makes these walks different is their personal style, the delightful details and excellent photographs, which combine to make this a unique book to keep and pore over.

£8.99

Walks in the Footsteps of Cornish Writers
Sue Kittow

Walks in the Footsteps of Cornish Writers features 20 walks each associated with different writers connected to Cornwall. It has been fascinating talking to the contemporary authors about their favourite walks. Similarly, it has been interesting to find out more about the places that were so special to those well known writers who are no longer with us - and why they were so special.

Some writers, like John Betjeman, have made their favourite places famous through verse or novels. Others, like Philip Marsden, use regular walks as a valuable part of their writing day, and it has been a privilege to share their thoughts. From Derek Tangye's books based in Lamorna to the Reverend Stephen Hawker at Morwenstow, here are a variety of walks that inspired the authors, and I hope will inspire readers too.

Each walk has an introduction, a factbox with all essential information, and details of maps, refreshments, history, points of interest and clear directions.
£8.99

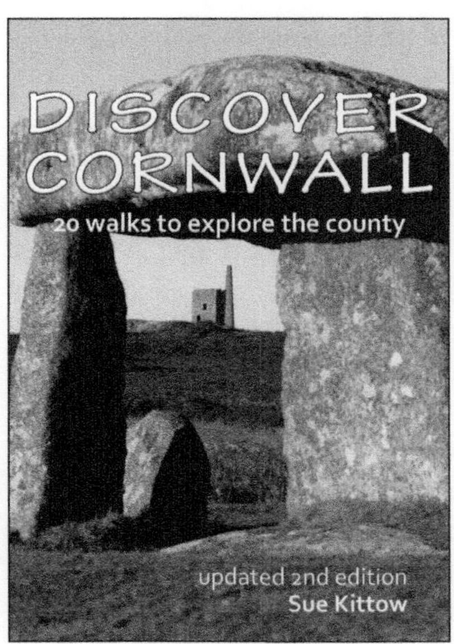

Discover Cornwall
20 walks to explore the county
Sue Kittow

Cornwall's fine golden sands have provided the backdrop for many childhood holidays, but it is also a coastal footpath, there are numerous less known routes that are great fun to investigate.

There are a good range of gentle to moderate walks between 4 and 6 miles in length. Discover Cornwall lists 20 walks providing a healthy and entertaining way to keep fit, learn about Cornwall, and enjoy the beaches, moorland and hisotry of this magical county.

The walks have clear directions, delightful details and excellent photographs, maing this a unique book to keep and pore over for readers as well as walkers.
£8.99

Rainy Days in Cornwall
Jean Patefield

Cornwall has a long and beautiful coastline, with wonderful beaches many of which are excellent for surfing. There are also picturesque valleys and woodland. Unfortunately, being in the west of England, even in high summer wind and rain can lash the beaches, the temperature can plummet and the coast can be shrouded in mist and drizzle. What should one do when your week's summer holiday is turning into a disaster? Carry on regardless, huddled behind a windbreak trying to keep warm or patronise the numerous attractions and spend a fortune? Rainy Days in Cornwall offers a solution to this problem with twenty suggestions of free and interesting things to do in Cornwall in less than perfect weather.
£8.99

Cornwall Walking on the level
Norman & June Buckley

This book selects and illustrates 28 routes, mainly circular, which explore some of the finest parts of the county, without serious ascent. In addition to the route directions, the distance, ascent, car parking, refreshment and map, with a succinct assessment, are provided for each walk.
£8.99